AWAKEN THE WARRIOR WITHIN

How to Take Back Control of Your Life, Double Your Confidence, and Get Everything You Want out of Life!

Tony Wolfe

Copyright © 2017 Tony Wolfe. All rights reserved. No portion of this book, except for brief review, may be reproduced, stored in a retrieval system, or transmitted in any form or by any means—electronic, mechanical, photocopying, recording, or otherwise—without the written permission of the publisher. For information contact Inspired Publishing Books.

Published by
Inspired Publishing Books
Inspired Publishing Ltd
27 Old Gloucester Street
London
WC1N 3AX

MEDICAL DISCLAIMER: The following information is intended for general information purposes only. Individuals should always see their health care provider before administering any suggestions made in this book. Any application of the material set forth in the following pages is at the reader's discretion and is his or her sole responsibility.

ISBN- 978-1-78555-014-0

DISCLAIMER

The writer of this material believes that a natural and holistic approach to health and maintaining a balance within the human body are of extreme importance in experiencing energy, vitality, and vibrant health throughout life.

The author recognizes that within the scientific and medical fields there are widely divergent viewpoints and opinions. This material is written for the express purpose of sharing educational information and scientific research gathered from the studies and experiences of the author, healthcare professionals, scientists, nutritionists and informed health advocates.

None of the information contained in this book is intended to diagnose, prevent, treat, or cure any disease, nor is it intended to prescribe any of the techniques, materials or concepts presented as a form of treatment for any illness or medical condition.

Before beginning any practice relating to health, diet or exercise, it is highly recommended that you first obtain the consent and advice of a licensed health care professional.

The author assumes no responsibility for the choices you make after your review of the information contained herein and your consultation with a licensed healthcare professional.

None of the statements in this book have been evaluated by the Food & Drug Administration (FDA) or the American Medical Association (AMA).

Acknowledgments

I want to thank my wife and daughters for your love, through the darkness and the light. I am the luckiest man alive.

To my parents and in-laws, thanks for always being there.

Thanks to my mentors, some I know personally, some only from books and seminars. You have all helped guide me in some aspect of my life from near and afar: Mark Anastasi, Joel Bauer, Matt Episcopo, Tim Ferris, Anthony Robbins and Robin Sharma.

Thanks to everyone who helped me on my journey back to health, and who guided me in my quest to awaken my Warrior within ... you helped me find my true purpose in life and my mission is to pay it forward.

Thanks to Mr. Sam Estrabillo for the Warrior artwork, you are a tremendously talented individual.

Thanks to my editor Ameesha Green, your ability to sift through the fluff and help hone precision was invaluable.

Thank you to the universe and all the wondrous powers that be.

Peace, Health and Happiness!

Tony

Table of Contents

Introduction – The Secret Power Within You	1
Why I Wrote This Book	5
What has happened to us	5
What causes us to wear down – physically, mentally emotionally and spiritually?	7
My Warrior within awakening experience	11
The purpose of this book	15
Chapter 1 – The Way of the Warrior	17
Why do we need to awaken the warrior within?	18
What is the Warrior within?	20
What is a true Warrior?	21
The Warrior's Code	23
What do Warriors do and think? The way of the Warrior	26
What will change for you if you follow the way of the Warrior	32
How do we awaken the Warrior within?	32
Chapter 2 – Finding Your Warrior's Passion and Purpose	35
Discover your values	38
Crystallize your values	45
Incorporating these values into your life	47
Removing energy drainers	49
Delegation and elimination	50

What feels right to you?	52
Every Warrior needs a mission	53
Your Warrior needs to go on a quest	55

Chapter 3 – Strengthening Your Warrior's Mind — 59

How do you start your day?	60
Are you thinking self-defeating thoughts?	61
How do you rewire your mind and change your thinking?	63
Where focus goes, energy flows	64
Don't allow yourself to play the victim card	67
Fight or flight	68
Change your state	71
Take care of your mind	79

Chapter 4 – Fueling Your Warrior Within — 83

The 2 billion year old car metaphor	84
What are the obstacles to eating healthy?	85
Food is medicine	88
Some general tips on eating	90
Some handy tips on *how* to eat	94
The Top 12 superfoods that can heal your entire body	96

Chapter 5 – Moving and Rejuvenating Your Warrior Within — 99

Why you need to rejuvenate	100
Negative effects of not enough sleep	101
Setting up your work day to rejuvenate yourself	108

Moving your body	111
Chapter 6 – Energizing Your Warrior Within	115
Energy in our bodies	116
What is Qi or universal energy?	117
Energy is all around us	118
How does it feel when your Qi is healthy and balanced	121
What causes your Qi to stagnate, stop flowing or deplete?	122
What increases, strengthens and balances Qi?	125
Qi and Martial Arts	128
Reiki and Energy	131
Science and Energy	134
Fill your body with good energy!	134
Chapter 7 – The Awakened Warrior and Beyond!	137
Taking stock of where we are	138
Make the decision	139
Your new future	140
Earning more money	143
Attracting your soulmate	148
The Awakened Warrior and beyond: thoughts to guide you in your new life	150
You are the Warrior you have awakened	152
You are doing what 99% of the world is not	153
21 Day Awaken the Warrior Within Challenge	154

Introduction - The Secret Power within You!

There is a secret power hidden deep within you.

It is a force so powerful that once unleashed, it will enable you to take control of your life, to increase your self-confidence, to live a life of passion and purpose; it will give you the strength, skills, and courage to allow you to get anything you want out of life.

This power is called the Warrior within.

The sad thing is that many people do not even realize it is there! It has lain there dormant, for years, maybe decades. Their inner Warrior has been hidden from them … buried deep down, covered by stress, hectic lifestyles, polluted water, social media, food void of nutrition, frustration, sadness, or a sedentary lifestyle.

This book will show you:

- What the Warrior within is
- How to awaken *your* Warrior
- How to keep your Warrior healthy
- How to keep your Warrior energized
- How you will feel once your Warrior is awakened
- What you will be capable of once your Warrior is awakened
- How to ensure your Warrior remains awakened

You deserve to wake up smiling, happy to start the day, excited about life, and full of energy and passion! Yet as much as you deserve it, sometimes waking up feels more like a battle just to get your body moving.

Wouldn't you *love* to jump out of bed in the morning and happily shout to the world...

- ✓ I wake up every day with a huge smile on my face, eager to take on my day!
- ✓ I am filled with positive self-confidence and make decisions easily!
- ✓ I am with the person of my dreams!
- ✓ I radiate with good health!
- ✓ I live with passion and purpose!
- ✓ I earn the money I am worth!
- ✓ I feel great! I feel happy! I am amazing!
- ✓ I make a difference in the world!

The fact is that it's not hard to do—in fact, anyone can do it. *But you need to know how to do it.* And that is what this book is all about. This book was written with one single purpose—to help *you* feel great. This is **your** instruction manual to feeling *great* ... You are exactly where you need to be, right here, right now. Nothing happens by chance in this world, and the fact that you are reading this book, out of all the millions of books out there, means it is your destiny to succeed.

You might feel like it is not your destiny to succeed. Indeed, many people choose to continue to live a life on half speed. It has been drilled into them to blindly accept what they are told. They are told, and sadly believe, that the whole purpose of the week is just to survive, just to get through it. That living from paycheck to paycheck and being stressed out financially is just a fact of life ... they had better just get used to it. They have been told that there is no sense in really trying to live the life of their dreams because odds are that they will fail, so why bother even trying? *But it does not have to be like this!*

Like so many people I talk to, I have been roughed up a bit by life. I have suffered some health issues, personal tragedy, lack of energy and passion, mild depression, and found myself wondering what my purpose was in life. I was down, but as I discovered, I was not out. 20 years ago, I made the decision to see whether there was more to life than just feeling like I was surviving. I wanted to see whether I could rekindle my flame of passion and excitement, whether my body could feel healthier, whether I could have more energy, smile more, sleep better at night, and wake up feeling rested.

I wanted to see whether I could feel like I used to when I was younger—more alive, less cynical, and full of hope. So I went on a journey to see whether this was possible. Over the past two decades, I have spent tens of thousands of dollars exploring, experimenting with, and discovering some amazing and beautiful things on my journey to bring myself back to physical, emotional, and spiritual health. To awaken the Warrior within that had been slumbering. The journey has been amazing! And the great thing is that you don't need to spend the same tens of thousands of dollars, because I am going to share with you, right here in this book, everything that I have learned!

This book is here to save you the 20-year learning curve that I had to go through to regain my health, confidence, passion, and power ... so that you don't have to go through what I went through. I want you to be able to feel better now, not 20 years from now. This book is written for you, and it is straight from my heart. It can be a powerful tool for you, and I am excited to hear about all the great things it will help you to unleash within yourself!

It is time for your Warrior to awaken!

Making the decision

If you're struggling to make the decision to change, watch *The Secret Life of Walter Mitty*.

The movie shows one man's journey to regain the life he was meant to lead. Walter Mitty constantly daydreams of a life where he is confident, happy, heroic, a warrior ... all the things he does *not* believe he is. In real life, he is meekly going through the motions at work and in general. He is not happy, has no self-confidence, lets his new boss walk all over him, is afraid to ask out the girls of his dreams, and is afraid to step out and actually let himself shine.

Then, a series of events push Walter into a situation where his back is against the wall at work ... and at 36:30 of the movie (by my calculations), *something* happens in Walter's mind. Something is unleashed within Walter. **He makes a decision.** And he goes on a mission that takes him halfway across the globe ... to awaken the Warrior within him.

When he returns, people can't help but sense a huge difference in him. They view him and talk to him in a very different way, and in return he does and says things that only would have happened in his daydreams before. He is a man completely transformed. He is happy, confident, more outgoing; he smiles, he starts dating the woman of his dreams, he walks with a quiet swagger in his step, and he just has this "sense" about him. This power is within you too. It is waiting to be awakened. The Warrior within you is waiting to emerge!

Everything in life starts with a decision: the "cutting off" of any other options. You just need to make that decision ... the decision to awaken your Warrior within.

Why I Wrote This Book

What has happened to us?

Every day, I see so many people wandering aimlessly, a blank expression on their face, too busy typing on their cellphones, rushing through life, never taking the time to stop and smell the roses, not even looking up to meet the eyes of those around them. They spend too much time at work or in transit to and fro. They pop pills for backaches and headaches. They have lost the quality time with their families that they want and they need. They seldom stop to recharge their batteries and so they feel tired most of the time. They seem as if they are living life on autopilot, or are perhaps just feeling lost.

In my research, I have discovered that so many of us have settled—settled for a life that deep inside, we know does not fulfill us; settled on believing that each day is something to just survive, rather than wishing it would never end. When did it become natural to not feel excited about the future? To keep hitting the snooze button on the alarm clock and eventually having to drag ourselves out of bed? To not be happy? To feel powerless? To be stressed, sick, tired, depressed, to constantly worry? Or worse yet, to feel so beaten down that we feel nothing at all, or to be made to feel by others that our opinions and wishes don't matter? To feel powerless to change the world.

If you are reading this, chances are you have felt this way at least once in your life, or you know someone who has experienced it.

Although many people do not talk about it, and are often afraid to even admit it to themselves, unfortunately what you are feeling has become *common* in today's world! There IS a reason for why you are feeling this way. And you need to realize that you are not alone. **The mission of this book is to help you understand why it is happening, and give you a precise, quick, easy, and powerful solution to break out of it!** Everyone can do it. **You** can do it. And it can be done quicker than you might expect.

I know it can be done because I went through this myself. I have empathy for those who feel that somehow the life they are living is not all it should be, because I used to feel this way. I lost my health. My wife and I suffered a personal tragedy. I was constantly sick. Constantly on antibiotic after antibiotic. I was depressed. I had no energy. I lost my zest, my passion. I existed, but did not feel alive. I felt like I was there ... but not really. I was not the man I wanted to be for my family. There was something missing. I felt like I fell into a darkness.

But then I discovered something that helped me find **me** again, the **me** that I thought had vanished. And it is time for you to re-ignite your passion, your purpose, your confidence, your smile, your swagger, your love for life, and your desire. It is time for your Warrior within to **rise** and to go out and fully and gleefully challenge life for all that it has to offer!

The timing of this book is critical because we as people, as men and women, are at a crossroads; we are at a turning point. Something needs to change. Now. We cannot keep going down the same beaten path, because it is literally killing us. It is smothering who we are, who we have been, and it is replacing it, replacing us ... you and me ... with a bland, generic, pathetic version of who we could be. We are becoming a society without honour, passion, a code for living, or a purpose for being. Our bodies are becoming obese and our lifestyle sedentary. Kids are constantly hooked up to phones or video games and their attention span has diminished to the point where it is hard for them to focus on one thing for too long without getting antsy. Many people feel trapped with no way out. We are becoming lost.

Before we get to the solutions to bring a better you, let's first look at the traps that life seems to have fallen into for so many. See whether you connect with any of them, and whether you have experienced any of this yourself.

What causes us to wear down—physically, mentally, emotionally, and spiritually?

Advertisers tell us that we **must** consume. We must buy things. We must keep accumulating more and more. That is the only way we will ever be happy. Advertising has manipulated us to buy what they want, to make *them* rich, even as it harms us. Advertising has infiltrated our society and boldly steered us in directions we shouldn't be going ... and most of the time we don't even realize it is happening! Make no mistake about it, advertising has one intention, and one intention only: to sway you away from your own beliefs and values, and have you adapt the beliefs and values that *they* want you to have.

We are told we need instant gratification. If we cannot afford something, then we are told the solution is to just put it on a credit card. We need it now! Never mind the fact that financial debt is one of the major causes of stress today.

We're told to just keep pushing everything further and further down the road. Have you ever looked at the US debt clock? This is a very graphic example of what is happening in many people's lives as we speak (On a much smaller scale). You can find it at http://www.usdebtclock.org/.

There is no longer a need for any kind of temporary discomfort. If you are sick, then you need to take some kind of medication that will provide instant relief. If you have just eaten greasy pizza, a huge soda pop, and cheese nachos, there is no reason you need to feel indigestion. Simply take this drug and keep stuffing your face. There is no need to worry about any potential side effects, which many times seem to be much worse than whatever our original problem is. There are so many amazingly powerful all-natural, drug-free ways to heal ourselves, yet so many people are unaware of them.

The food we eat is often filled with chemicals. It pollutes our bodies and minds. It is fast, it is convenient, it is cheap, and it is killing us! According to an OECD 2014 report, 1 in 3 adults in the USA, Mexico, and New Zealand, and 1 in 4 adults in Canada, Australia, Chile, and Hungary are obese. Being obese is not just a cosmetic problem—it can greatly raise your risk of numerous other health problems such as heart disease, high blood pressure, stroke, and type 2 diabetes to name but a few.

Much of our food is no longer natural. It is man-made, with much of the nutrients processed right out of it so that it will last longer and look prettier. They are even creating new "foods" using GMOs (Genetically Modified Organisms), and no one really can say how these foods will affect us over time. Our water supply is filled with chemicals and pollutants.

Many of us have lost contact with nature, with mother earth. So many of us live in concrete cities with hardly any trees. Hardly any grass. Hardly any flowers. Hardly any nature. We rarely spend time in nature, and seldom go outside except to walk to the bus or the car. It is no wonder that people feel so lost. Our past ancestors spent their entire lives in the fields and forest, on the water, in the sunshine, breathing in fresh air. Now we breathe in smog and pollution. Nature has a beautiful calming energy to it, it helps us to naturally de-stress. It is a gift to us, and it allows us to absorb its beautiful peacefulness. However when we lose touch with it, we lose that connection to mother earth—we lose that connection to peacefulness.

One of the reasons so many people suffer from anxiety, depression, and illness is because they do not have that natural connection any more. Instead they are surrounded by concrete, loud noises, flashing lights, and cars spitting pollution in to the air we breathe and the water we drink.

Many of us don't take good care of our physical bodies anymore. Our jobs involve sitting at a desk hunched over, staring at a computer screen for eight to ten hours a day. We can drive to work. We take elevators and escalators. By the time we get home and drive the kids to sports practice or music lessons, we are too tired to get any exercise for ourselves. We can't keep going like this.

And mentally, we may be more stressed out than at any time in history. Many people say they are so busy, they have no down time. Financial worry eats away at people. Insomnia is rampant. Stress affects each of our bodies in different ways, but excess stress is generally a cause of disease in most of us. It can cause so many illnesses, physically, mentally, and spiritually. Some of the side effects of stress may seem small at first, simply an inconvenience, but if left unchecked can lead to serious health issues and even death. Somehow people have to find a way to get some balance back in their lives.

We have become so busy. We are on the move so much that we seldom stop to smell the roses. Not only does our lifestyle cause us stress by us taking on too many things at once, but we don't slow down enough to ask ourselves whether we even enjoy what we are doing? Just like anything, if we don't stop to rest and recover, we risk burning ourselves out. I used to think I was indestructible until my health crashed. Many people are headed down the same road if they don't learn some simple secrets of self-care.

Many men have become lost. They are uncertain of what is expected of them anymore. What is the definition of a "real" man? There seems to be so many conflicting messages. The message from society is constantly changing depending who wants what from us. We have lost the ability to listen to ourselves, to our true beliefs, to our true inner self. This leads to confusion, to insecurity, and ultimately to stress and depression.

The messages that society gives us are often not good. Good news does not sell. If you look at the news today, it is difficult to find anything positive. Sensationalism sells. The images we are surrounded with are war, explosions, beheadings, robberies, murders. Politicians sling mud at each other, with nothing sacred any more. We become more and more desensitized to it all. What used to be rated restricted, for violence or sex, is now readily available for kids of ALL ages in things like music videos and video games! It is no wonder that we have lost our focus, our aim, our mission.

More, now than at any point in the history of the world, we need people to step up and reclaim their lives. To feel confident, to live with purpose and passion. It is time for you to cast off your fear, to cast off your doubt and your sadness.

It is time for you to step up and live the life you know you were meant to live.

It is time for you to awaken your Warrior within!

My Warrior within awakening experience

My story is not that unique. The more people I talk to in life, I find that so many people have had the same or worse happen to them. But I want to share this with you so that you can see where I have come from, and that no matter how low you may feel, there is always hope, the sun will always rise tomorrow no matter how dark the night may seem.

I was working at a job I loved, often in the office or out on the road 7 days a week. Many days I would leave my house at 7 am and return after midnight. I was always in a rush; run one more seminar, meet with one more client. In the past, I had always been quite physically active, but as I got busier at work, I decided I no longer had time for something as frivolous as exercise. I seldom prepared meals in advance and so I ate fast food almost every day, sometimes twice a day. My snacks increasingly became a search for a quick energy burst; something with sugar or caffeine in it; chocolate bars, pop, donuts. My body would get jacked up on sugar to get the energy for the next meeting, but then after a few hours, my body would come down from the sugar high, leaving me feeling so tired, so I had to go and get another quick sugar energy fix.

This cycle went on for years, and it wore down my overall health, energy, and immunity. I started getting sick frequently. Because I didn't feel I could afford to miss work, I continually went to my doctor demanding a quick fix ... antibiotics. My doctor warned me more than once that I needed to let myself get healthy. I didn't listen. It was an endless cycle of sickness followed by new antibiotic ... again and again and again.

It was at that time that my amazing wife and I lost our first born daughter. I will never forget having to watch her be unhooked from life support. How can any parent have to make this decision? How could this be? How could this have happened? Why? Why us? I felt numb. I returned to work soon after, never really grieving, just not knowing what else to do. I had a new found energy; I was driven by an anger so deep inside me I didn't even realize it was there. But it was, and it began to eat away at me.

When our second daughter was almost two, my health finally gave out and my body crashed. I quit my job. I was fat, I was sick, I had no energy, I was depressed. I was at the lowest point of my life, and I decided that there must be more to life than that. And that is when I began my search, my quest to bring myself back to health.

Over the years that followed, I spent literally tens of thousands of dollars flying across the world, attending seminars, reading, watching videos, learning as much as I could. I went on a drum journey with a shaman. I sat with amazing men in sweat lodges. I changed my diet, stopped drinking cow's milk, and became a vegetarian. I tried different herbs, vitamins, and supplements.

I meditated. I was introduced to an amazing healing energy called Reiki (and I believe this helped save my life). I did the ancient exercises of Qigong and Tai Chi. I experimented with different power amulets. I enjoyed the peacefulness of bees wax candles and calming music. I experienced the healing prowess of essential oils. I learned the powerful affect that our mind and our thoughts can have on our health: physically, mentally, and spiritually. I went to a health spa.

I tried different types of exercises including daily walking and a very effective little tool called a rebounder. My wife and I went on a 5-day hike, stretching ourselves past what we thought were our limits. I learned how to clear out the negative in my life to open up more space for the positive. I studied Traditional Chinese Medicine (acupuncture, herbs, and energy work such as Qigong).

It has healed me and my family in many ways ... completely naturally, and so powerfully. I expanded the self-imposed boundaries of my life. I learned how to awaken my Warrior within.

What I learned gave me the courage, strength, and skills to overcome the other challenges that came my way in the following years. My appendix began leaking inside my body and was operated on just before bursting. My heart stopped on the operating table and I had to be shocked back to life. We bought a new house and I lost my job just weeks afterwards, challenging us financially. My heart went out of whack and I suffered from atrial fibrillation. I went through numerous painful and scary procedures. I was put on meds including blood thinner (rat poison). On and off for years, I was constantly out of breath, I couldn't exercise, I had no energy, I battled depression, and I wondered whether that twinge in my chest was a heart attack. There were numerous times I thought I was honestly going to die.

Those years were very challenging, certainly filled with lots of ups and downs, and they pushed me to my max sometimes. I knew that it could be overcome and that it would take all the skills and attitudes I had developed over the years to do it. As with before, I kept reaching out to see what more there was out there. I kept trying new things, experiencing life, seeing what connected with me.

And as with every other time in life ... a new day came.

With the help of my family and friends and the wisdom gained from alternative health practitioners, I regained my health. The Warrior within me that I had allowed to be buried so deeply under years of stress, poor diet, lack of exercise, health problems, and depression ... buried so deeply that I didn't even know it was there any more ... *this Warrior finally crawled out of the wreckage and took a magnificent and deep breath in!*

I went biking again, I played basketball again, and went for long hikes in the woods. I had persevered. I moved forward in life, and I started sharing with others, in person, and through my blog, all the things I had learned so that they could begin to feel alive again too. I am committed to living life to the fullest, and I want to share this with you!

I am not a superstar. I don't have six pack abs. I am just a normal guy who got beat down in life, suffered from depression and illness, but brushed himself off and got back up ... and now I LOVE my life and feel like one of the luckiest men on the planet!

If you are feeling a little run down, if you are feeling like you have lost your passion or your zest, if you wish that you could feel like you used to feel, I KNOW that you can do it.

Over the remainder of this book and this journey, I will share with you many tips, thoughts, and ideas that you can use to get your engine revved up again! I have learned from some amazing people; I have had some fabulous mentors and teachers ... and now I'd love to teach you!

The purpose of this book

We need heroes who can rise above this lethargy sweeping the world.
We need people with character, honesty, and integrity to help rebalance the world.
We need people to lead by example. To live a life filled with purpose and passion.
We need Warriors!

We need to awaken the Warrior within.

That is the purpose of this book.
- To awaken your Warrior.
- To empower you.
- To help you find your inner balance again.
- To find your confidence in this world again.
- To allow you to stride into a room again with a confidence, with a presence, with a sense of self.
- To allow you to radiate with a fire that other people will be drawn to.
- To give your voice volume, and allow your own unique voice to be heard.
- To allow you to wake up in the morning and jump out of bed with excitement for the day to come.
- To find your purpose in life and make sure you weave that purpose into your day-to-day life.
- To be on fire with desire!
- To feel that passion again!
- To allow you keep your chin up, puff out your chest, and to shine gloriously!

It is time to awaken the Warrior within—your Warrior within!

The following chapters are going to give you ALL the tools you need to awaken your inner Warrior and feel alive again! *They are coming right from my heart to you.* You are in a good place, everything you need is right here. At times you might be so pumped up you want to skip ahead to the end and start your 21 day Warrior Challenge … but I encourage you to read all the chapters first, they will give you a solid foundation on which to build your new life! And then in the final chapter a fuse will be lit under you, one that will launch you onwards and upwards, and I will issue you your 21 day Warrior challenge! I am so excited for you! What you will be learning and doing has the power to change your life!

So strap on your sword, batten down the hatches, and get ready to rumble!

Are you ready?
I can't hear you!
I said ARE YOU READY?

Ok! Let's do this!

CHAPTER 1:

The Way of the Warrior

"Warriors do not lower themselves to the standards of other people; they live independently according to their own standards and code of honour."
Bohdi Sanders, Modern Bushido: Living a Life of Excellence

In this chapter, we'll look at:
- WHY do we need to awaken the Warrior within?
- What is the Warrior within?
- What code does a Warrior live by?
- What does a Warrior do?
- How does a Warrior think?
- What are some real-life examples of Warriors?
- How do we awaken our Warrior?

Before we delve into what exactly it is, we had better consider some words of warning...

CAUTION: When you do awaken your Warrior within, and follow the way of the Warrior, here is what you can expect could potentially happen to you

- You will feel more alive.
- You will smile more.
- You will sleep better.
- You will wake up and feel more rested and rejuvenated.
- You will feel more in shape.
- You will enjoy work more.
- You will make more money.
- You will enjoy your family more.
- You will enjoy life more.
- You will feel more energy.
- You will walk with a bounce in your step.
- You will walk into a room and people will take notice.
- You will be more productive.
- You will feel more balanced.
- You will attract that special person you want in your life.
- You will feel like you have a purpose in life.
- You will feel more confident.
- You will appreciate the little things again.
- You will feel supremely happy!

Does this list sound good to you? These are just some of the potential benefits you could enjoy!

So let's dig in.

Why do we need to awaken the Warrior within?

We are all born perfect. We start life with unlimited potential. We can all become anything we want, we can all live our life any way we want ... anything is possible. Then, gradually, the powers that be start to define FOR us how they think we should act, who we should be, who we should have as friends, what our interests should be. These powers that be could be anyone in power from parents to school teachers to coaches to politicians to employers to advertisers. I am not saying that these sources are bad, but they all have their opinions, they all have their reasons, and even if they are doing something they feel is an effort to protect us, they are still influencing us. Many times, they are influencing us to do good things, things that will benefit us ... but sometimes we are influenced to do things that hold us down.

Some adults were told by their teachers when they were younger that they would never amount to anything. Some people use that as a spring board to prove their teachers wrong ... but many do not. Those that don't then live their lives with a huge uncertainty gnawing away at them deep in their gut, and it affects everything they do, every decision they make. It causes doubt and indecision.

We are told *NO, we can't do that. We shouldn't go there. We shouldn't hang out with those people. That's not possible. Only the rich can do that. You will never be wealthy. You will never get that job.* We hear many of these things countless times in our lives. Some people will maliciously be negative to your goals and dreams. Some people who feel that they have not made it in life don't want to lose you as a friend, so they put down any attempted thought you have of realizing your true potential.

Little by little, life can start to wear on us. We may not even realize it at the time, but it adds up—starting early in your childhood and continuing on through adulthood. Kids at school made fun of you and made you cry. The refs made a bad call in your game. You didn't get into that course you wanted. Someone else got the promotion you wanted and felt you deserved. Your car broke down on the side of the road. Your child is sick. Your house needs new shingles and you don't know how you can afford them. Your back aches every night and it is hard to get to sleep. You just found out your spouse cheated on you. Someone close to you passed away. Things happen to all of us.

So that once beautiful inner brilliance begins to get bogged down. Deep inside of us, doubts have grown about our abilities. We have developed fears. For example, the fear of failure. What happens if we really go all out at something and we don't succeed? How embarrassing would that be? And how terrifying would that be? That one fear paralyzes countless people from even trying something that they would dearly love to do!

Do you know anyone who thought it would be good to start their own small business, but the fear of failure stopped them from even trying? That once unlimited potential suddenly now has limits.

Do you know anyone who gave up on a dream and locked themselves into a life that gave them a more reliable paycheck yes, but deep inside they felt somewhat empty and incomplete.

Imagine how it would feel to follow your heart and YOUR desires. Imagine how it would feel to be totally in tune with your purpose in life, to find passion in what you do. Imagine the joy!

What is the Warrior within?

The Warrior within is your true inner self. *It is who* **you** *really are ... not who the world tells you that you should be.* It has been inside you all your life. When you were born, the Warrior was you. You were the Warrior. It was synchronized. It was in unity. It could shine. However, little by little, the Warrior got buried and lulled to sleep.

When you find your Warrior again and awaken it, it is really you connecting with who you are supposed to be! You will clearly see your purpose in life, and your life and your purpose will be aligned. It is very invigorating!

All the fear and self-doubt that has built up over the years eats away at your self-confidence. You begin to lack the vision of what things will look like in the future; your vision becomes restricted to just the immediate future. It reduces your "stick-to-it-ness", and so it reduces your ability and desire to be persistent and see things through. This means that you may get excited about something, and start to do it, but the moment you are met with an obstacle, if you don't overcome it **immediately** (because remember we are now a society where things have to be instantaneous), then you become disheartened and give up.

The Warrior within you is what gives you the inner strength, the inner confidence, and the inner vision to not only see what the end result can look like, but gives you the **heart** to keep plugging away until you reach your goal! It is immensely satisfying. And every time you accomplish something, it strengthens your whole being, and you shine brighter.

What is a true Warrior?

When you think of a Warrior, what do you think of? Who do you think of?

Let me be clear about what I think a Warrior is not. Just because someone is physically massive or physically superior, that alone does not make them a Warrior. Just because someone has won victories it does not mean they are a Warrior. Someone who enjoys harming, or harms just because they can is not a Warrior. A Warrior is not cruel. A Warrior is not a bully. A Warrior does not take advantage of helpless people. A Warrior is not consumed and driven by rage, or by greed.

In my opinion, the concept of the true Warrior is being misrepresented in society today. It is misrepresented in video games where so many games are just about violence ... and our children play these at such young ages. In music, just because someone can make a fast buck, too many unscrupulous people are billed as heroes, despite the dubious subjects and concepts that their music is about.

Here is a partial list of characteristics that all *true* Warriors share:
- A Warrior's word is their bond.
- A Warrior constantly trains, prepares, and puts in the necessary effort. They know there are no shortcuts.
- A Warrior displays selflessness.
- A Warrior can experience fear, but fear will not stop them from doing what they know is right.
- A Warrior is generous.
- A Warrior helps others.
- A Warrior knows how important their honor is.
- A Warrior always displays compassion.
- A Warrior has faith, and they have a belief in something bigger than their self.
- A Warrior realizes the importance of and works on their physical strength and endurance.
- A Warrior has definiteness of purpose. They are on a mission.

- A Warrior takes care of themselves. They eat right. They rejuvenate their body, mind, and soul.
- A Warrior doesn't put stuff off; they meet things head on.
- A Warrior practices awareness; they get to know themselves, their strengths, and things they need to work on.
- A Warrior has courage.
- A Warrior practices discipline.
- A Warrior is not afraid to love.
- A Warrior respects and honors women and other men.
- A Warrior is loyal to their friends.
- A Warrior is adaptable.
- A Warrior is a minimalist; they do not need to measure their wealth in "things".
- A Warrior is decisive.
- A Warrior leads by example. Always.

> **TO DO:**
> Review the list of characteristics that Warriors have. Put a check mark beside the qualities that you feel you are very strong in, and then put a circle around those that you feel you need to work on. Feel free to add your own ideas and thoughts to your list.

The Warrior's Code

The most famous Warriors all have a code that they live by. This is a set of rules and guidelines that they adhere to in life. It is clear, well-defined, and allows a Warrior to always make the right choice in how to live their life. This clarity and certainty allows them to be happier.

In Europe of old, there were the Knights who lived by a code of chivalry. This was a moral system that emphasized such things as bravery, courtesy, honor, and great gallantry toward women.

Another very famous code was used by the Samurai of ancient Japan. It was called Bushido, and literally translated to "the Way of the Warrior". I have always been drawn to many of the ideals of the Samurai, and used their concepts in business. Anyone can benefit from adapting the Bushido into their life, so let's look at the concept in more detail.

Bushido - The Way of the Warrior

The Samurai code was an unwritten code that consisted of several rules or guidelines; it was really a code of moral principles. A Samurai had to adhere to all the aspects of the code, and live their lives completely in unity with the code, or they were not allowed to be viewed as a Samurai. Their code was not something they could slide in and out of—it was totally ingrained in every aspect of their life.

Imagine how much simpler life would become if you had a set of rules or guidelines that you always lived by. Every time you had a decision to make, you weighed it against your code. If it did not align with the code, you didn't do it. Simple. Imagine the power of that. Well, to awaken your Warrior within, strengthen it, and keep it strong, include this code in your life!

Although generally an unwritten code, there are seven aspects mentioned in "Bushido: The Soul of Japan", by Nitobe Inazo.

1. Integrity. This can also be viewed as justice or rectitude (morally correct behavior, or righteousness). Integrity means doing the right thing, even when you are by yourself with no one watching. It is a straight and narrow path that a man should take. It means doing the right thing for the right reason. The Samurai loathed people who did not keep their word.

2. *Courage and bravery.* Confucius said "Courage is perceiving what is right, and doing it not argues lack of courage ". It is a calm presence of mind; it is composure under pressure, even on the battlefield. Samurais sought to show courage every day, in every action, in every moment, whether they were in danger or not.

3. *Benevolence.* This means to show kindness and compassion to everything and everyone regardless of the situation. As Inazo said: "The bravest are the tenderest, the loving are the daring".

4. *Politeness.* Politeness is not good if the only reason you are doing it is out of fear of offending someone. It should come as a result of a natural caring for others. Inazo says "In its highest form, politeness almost approached love".

5. *Honesty.* You demonstrate honesty not only through the words you speak, but by your actions as well. The word of the Samurai was his bond, and did not require anything to be written down. Habitual truthfulness was the way the Samurai lived.

6. *Honor.* Honor is associated with one's name; it is the basis of one's reputation. Honor is immortal, it is one's name, one's spirit, and it lived on well past the death of a Warrior.

7. *Loyalty.* This means to be trustful, and show this unconditionally not only to others, but to themselves as well. Loyalty is a treasure.

For a Warrior to live by the code they must: do the right thing for the right reasons; calmly show courage and bravery in all instances of life; show kindness and compassion to every living thing; to be polite to others as a result of truly caring for them; to be honest not only with what you say but also how you act; to be a man of honour, to have this as your reputation; and to be loyal to yourself and to others.

This code is broken so often and so rarely followed by many in the world today that if YOU were to abide by these, and make these a part of your life, you would truly stand out! You would shine.

> **TO DO:**
> Review The Bushido Code. Rewrite it for yourself (or download from my website) and hang it up on your wall where you will see it every day! You can even use it as a screen saver on your computer or phone.

What do Warriors do and think? The way of the Warrior

According to John Newman in his influential book "Bushido – The Way of the Warrior", the Bushido code not only related to a Samurai's physical actions, but more importantly with their inner spirit. The code was "an attempt to inculcate the men of power with a sense of responsibility and kindness, as well as physical and moral courage". The Samurai were not only physically gifted Warriors, but they were well educated, and patrons of the arts. A number of Warriors were talented writers and poets.

Balance

How different is that from what many perceive the definition of a Warrior to be today! It is no wonder our world is in trouble these days. People are so unbalanced: focusing on just one thing over others, a workaholic to the exclusion of their family, an extreme athlete to the exclusion of their mental abilities. A true warrior is someone who is well balanced in all aspects of life. This is what YOU need to get back to ... to every day strive to gain more balance in every aspect of your life.

In Chinese medicine, **balance** is the key to everything. The concept of yin and yang is simply a concept of balance, between the cold and the warm, the dark and the light. For a person to be healthy, they must be in balance both mentally and physically. To be the best Warrior you can be, you need to ensure that you are balanced, and that all parts of you are developed.

So a real Warrior is about much more than just physical strength or ability to wreak havoc on a battle field. A **true** Warrior is a very well-rounded person; one who does not just act out of anger or vengeance.

> What areas of your life do you need more balance in? **?**

Sportsmanship

The way of the Warrior is not regarded as an end result of winning or losing. It is regarded as the competition itself, the event itself, and the action of striving for something bigger than victory. You can compare Bushido to the concept of sportsmanship. A true sportsman can enjoy the game, and keep calm, gracious, and humble ... regardless of whether they win or lose. Winning or losing is not their measure of victory!

Loving life

A true Warrior loves their life because they can appreciate that it has to be about more than just the outcomes of life. It is about how you live life. Not just about the actions, but how you achieve them.

Awakening your Warrior inside means actually loving living life. It means appreciating the journey with eyes wide open, not just rushing to get to the end with your head down. The old saying about stopping to smell the roses is true. There are so many amazing things in the world, so many wonders, and yet it is so easy to drift through life in a daze ... alive but not really living.

Bettering yourself

The Samurai spent a lot of time bettering themselves in all aspects of life. Not only were they constantly training their bodies physically, practicing their fighting skills though repetition of movement in fighting, they also invested a lot of time and energy into training their mind. These Warriors incorporated ideas from Zen (which was part of the original Buddhism). One of the well accepted results of successful Zen practice was the ability of the Warrior to gain freedom from the *fear* of death. Imagine if we could truly free ourselves from our fears, how powerful would that make us? What things would we actually do, that currently we hesitate from doing because we are afraid of what would happen if we failed?

Controlling one's own mind

The Samurai realized how important state of mind was to their success on the battlefield. That is why they spent time learning things to free themselves from the self-limiting claws of fear. They also realized how important it was to be able to be calm, especially in the face of stress and danger. Fear can physically paralyze us so that even the most skilled swordsman could lose a battle to a lesser opponent if they could not control their own mind. To be at our best, we need to be relaxed and able to flow freely.

The Samurai practiced something called the Japanese Tea Ceremony, which involved a very particular method of preparing green tea, with precise movements. The process was very intense and required the Samurai to focus intently, and to remain calm and fluid in movements. It was a powerful tool to train their mind. The Samurai would practice this ceremony just before going into battle, and even sometimes during a lull in the battle.

Can you imagine getting ready to go into battle? Getting ready to face potential death ... by making tea? Look at our lifestyle today. We think our life is stressful because we have to make a presentation at work, or the hydro bill is more than we thought it would be ... or they ran out of our favorite drink at the supermarket. We allow stress to build up in us, and not release it. We feel like we are so busy. We keep moving, moving, moving ... seldom taking the time to stop and take an actual deep breath. We get sick. We get depressed. We seldom take the time to quiet our mind and really focus. What can we learn from the Samurai act of practicing the Japanese Tea Ceremony?

A Warrior lives in the <u>now</u>

A Warrior realizes that he must live in the <u>now</u>. Too many people live in the past, replaying old self-limiting movies in their minds of times when things didn't go as well as they would have liked. And even worse is when people take these "failures" from the past and project them into the future! People worry about what "might" happen, what "could" go wrong. Paralysis by analysis. You cannot allow the fear of the unknown to stop you from acting. You cannot allow things that happened in the past to colour your outlook of the future.

A wise warrior once told me, "There is no use in worrying, because by the time the things you are worrying about arrive, the very thing you are worrying about will have already been taken care of".

Warriors make a stand

"Every now and then, some place, sometime, you are going to have to plant your feet, stand firm and make a point of you are and what you believe in"
– Pat Riley

As a Warrior, sometimes you need to set your feet and take a stand. What do you believe in? What lines **won't** you cross?

In his book "The Way of the Seal", Mark Divine, a former navy seal, talks about the concept of a set point. Your set point is the point at which you make a stand, and you will not deviate from. It is something that ties into your purpose in life. A line you will not cross. It can be used to help you make a decision, because you know that if the situation is asking you to move off your set point, that you easily say no. If you are in business, your base line might be that you will always do what is right for your client.

In life you will be faced with many choices, and different people will try to sway you depending on what they want out of the scenario. Deep inside, you have to know what is right for you. Remember you need to stay in tune with who you are, and your actions have to be congruent with your beliefs. If you know in your heart one thing but behave in a different way, you will feel a darkness inside of you; you will self-sabotage your Warrior within.

A Warrior adds value

A Warrior doesn't just take from the world. A Warrior gives back to the world. A Warrior **adds value** to the world. What gift do you have that you can share with the world? It could be to earn income, or it could be to just give without any expectations. We all have something special inside of ourselves that the world needs more of. What is within you that can add value to the world? Find it. And share it. You will gain an incredible feeling from it.

Imagine your future

When you look to your own future, to your new life, you need to mentally allow yourself a chance to move forward with a fresh start. Picture your past as an old building, with the paint peeling, and an overgrown, ragged garden in front. You need to mentally tear that building down, to clear off the lot everything that once stood there, and leave behind ONLY a completely blank lot. You remove the past that is holding you back and now there is a magnificent field of nothingness.

On top of this void, you can now build **anything** you want! It is completely wide open! It is totally up to you... not what others want. This is your field, your future. Open your mind, use your imagination, be creative. Allow your mind to fill with wonder and awe. A Warrior lives right now. They are not held back by the mishaps of the past, nor the fear of the future. They redefine their new life each and every day.

What will change for you if you follow the way of the Warrior?

The Samurai were on a constant and never-ending mission of exploration and self-improvement, to free themselves from all the unnecessary distractions in life that can un-focus a person and deplete their energy. To awaken your Warrior, you need to awaken all areas of yourself, and to do that you need to explore all areas of yourself.

Awakening your Warrior and following the way of the Warrior means connecting with your true self, your true values. It means stop worrying and being fearful. It means stop focusing on yourself, your woes, and instead, focus on helping others, on creating value for others. Having a code to live by will give you a sense of stability, a sense of connectedness. It will empower you.

People strive for security, but when people keep flickering from one thing to another, from one idea to another, it makes them feel insecure. When you fully connect your life to your passion and purpose, you will be able to clearly see the course in life you need to take, and an amazing feeling of stability, and of quiet confidence will fall upon you. It will give you the ability to stick to things, to see them through.

How do we awaken the Warrior within?

The first thing you need to do though is to acknowledge that YOU do have a Warrior within you. Remember your Warrior may be very deeply buried from years of lack of use, and may be in a very weakened state. It may be very hard to sense, or even hard to believe you have such a powerful force within you ... but it is there! This is a critical thing. You have to **believe** that it is possible. That it could be there. It doesn't matter how you feel right now. Whether you are tired, or sick, or unmotivated, or feeling lost. It doesn't matter whether your self-confidence is at an all-time low, or the girl of your dreams won't even give you the time of day, you need to BELIEVE that the Warrior IS within YOU!

We are going to be looking at some things that may seem a little "strange" to you, mostly because they are not well known, and may be new to you...

Remember *everything happens for a reason.* You are here for a reason!

Start to see yourself as a Warrior. As a real-life Warrior. Think about it every day. Start to practice the principles, to make the principles part of your life, to live by the principles. Become the Warrior!

> **TO DO:**
> Make a list of people you view as true Warriors. They can come from any area of your life. You may know them personally, they may be someone you just know from afar, or they may be someone from the past. Write down all the reasons why you view them as Warriors. What about them really appeals to you, what things about them do you want to add into your life? Are there any things about them you want to ensure does not become part of your life?

CHAPTER 2: Finding Your Warrior's Passion and Purpose

"Don't ask yourself what the world needs; ask yourself what makes you come alive. And then go and do that. Because what the world needs is people who have come alive." - **Howard Thurman**

"There's no passion to be found playing small — in settling for a life that is less than you are capable of living." - **Nelson Mandela**

There are many aspects of your Warrior within that we must awaken. In this chapter, we will awaken the spiritual side of your Warrior. The word "spiritual" can mean different things to different people. To some it could mean a connection to their God, or a connection to a type of religion. I am using it in a different sense. By spiritual, I mean a connection with your spirit, with your higher **you**. I mean developing a self-awareness of who you really are, of what makes you tick, what makes you happy, what makes you fulfilled. The word "spirituality" actually comes from root words in Hebrew, Latin, and Greek that all mean wind, breath, or air—that which gives life. And that is what we are doing with your Warrior within—we are breathing life into it!

In this chapter, we'll look at spiritual aspects such as:
- Finding your passion and purpose in life.
- Discovering your values and aligning them with your life.
- Discovering your mission or quest.

So, we want to find your **passion** and your **purpose** in life. When you live your life doing what you love, then days fly by, and the world seems so much better. Unfortunately, so many people in the world find themselves locked in a life or a job that really doesn't satisfy them, and whether they realize it or not, it really detracts from their happiness in life. But when you are living a life truly **connected** to your passion and purpose, you allow your inner Warrior to emerge, to shine brightly, and you are filled with tremendous self-confidence and happiness!

One of the most vital parts of awakening your Warrior is to make sure that how you are living life is fully aligned with how you feel inside, with your beliefs and your values. When all these things are aligned, then life can be magical! When they are not, it can severely weaken your inner Warrior. This is one of the major reasons why people have lost their zest, why they get depressed and sick, why some people become zombies wandering aimlessly in life—because by not being in alignment, they feel like they have lost their way in life.

What about you? Ask yourself honestly. Is what you are doing in life perfectly aligned with how you see life, with your morals, your values? Does how you live your life, and the actions you take make you feel proud? Make you feel alive and energized?

Make you want to spring out of the bed so excited for a new day? The odds are not, or you wouldn't be reading this book.

One of the key things about a Warrior is that they know themselves. They know their strengths and their weaknesses. They know what **really** makes themselves tick. So before you can conquer the world, you need to first master yourself. This basic fact has been recognized for thousands of years by some of the wisest and most respected people of all time, such as influential Chinese philosopher Confucius, who said "He who conquers himself is the mightiest warrior."

So, a Warrior must spend time examining themselves—introspecting. This is something that most people in the world do not do! Many people try to analyze others, but do not spend the necessary time learning about themselves.

While you're doing these exercises, some powerful places to reflect on yourself and your life are:
- Going for a walk in nature
- Sitting in a calming place like a park
- Watching the waves roll in at the seashore
- On the treadmill while your energy is flowing
- Sitting listening to quiet music having a cup of coffee

Things to have with you:
- Bring a journal to write down all your important "Aha's"
- Have your phone or small digital recorder with you and record your thoughts

> **CONNECT:**
> Close your eyes for a second, look inwards, and see whether you can connect with it ... even if you can connect just for a second ... even if your Warrior has been beaten down so hard over the years, even if it feels like it is buried so deep ... know that you are on your way to bringing it back to the forefront of your life!

Discover your values

Values are your principles or standards of behavior. They are a central part of who you are and who you want to be. Just like the Samurai code, your values help the process of decision-making that much easier. Your values are in many ways your passions. So before we look at your passion and your purpose, let's start with some exercises to determine your values.

Start with some rough ideas, and then keep refining your answers until your hierarchy of values becomes so clear and feels so right that you know they are in alignment with your true Warrior within.

So roll up your sleeves and get ready to do some work. And never forget our mission as you read this book ... to awaken **your** Warrior! Keep picturing how awesome it will feel when you stride down the street, head held high, a smile on your face, knowing that you feel fully alive and in control of your life!

Think about and then answer the following 12 questions (you can download a worksheet from my website if it's easier):

1) What do you fill your personal space with?
Have you ever noticed that you keep things that are important to you where you can see them? Often they are put on display in obvious places for other to see, on the fireplace mantle, on

your desk at work, while things that are not really important to you end up in the garbage, or stuck in a box somewhere in a corner of the basement.

When you look around you, at your office or your home, what do you see? Family photos, sports trophies, business awards, books, souvenirs from vacations? What does your personal space say about your life? Do you have lots of comfortable furniture to entertain friends on? Are there movies or CDs or puzzles? Whatever you see around you is a very strong clue about what you value most.

Q: What are the top 3 things/ categories of things that fill your space?

_____

_____

_____

2) How do you spend your time?

Quite often, you will hear someone say that they don't have the time to do this or that. But the fact is that for the most part, people will always make the time to do the things that are really important to them, and run out of time for things that aren't. So if someone doesn't have the time for something, it is because they have not placed a high enough priority on it. And if something is judged as critically important, somehow they will find a way to make it fit in their schedule.

Q: What are the top 3 ways that you find yourself spending your time on?

_____

3) How do you spend your energy?

Have you ever noticed that you always have energy for those things you enjoy, that inspire you, that make you feel alive? Whereas things that are not aligned with your values, that you are not passionate about, often actually drain you of energy or you run out of energy even thinking about doing them? When you are doing something that you place great value on, you will still be energized even late at night, you often have more energy than before you even started that activity ... because you are doing something that you love and are inspired by. It is such an amazing difference. So how do you spend your energy, and where do you get your energy?

Q: In which 3 ways do you spend your energy and where/when/how do you feel energized?

_____

_____

4) How do you spend your money?

Like spending your energy, you usually always find money for things that are valuable to you, but you never want to part with your money for things that are not important to you. So the choices you make about how you spend your money can tell you a great deal about what you value most.

At this point, you may be noticing some overlap in your answers. Some of your answers to the questions of how you spend your time, energy, and money may have some of the same ideas. And that is good! It is healthy. It means that you have already found alignment in a lot of your values, goals, and daily activities. And if you notice that there are a lot of differences in your answers to the first four questions, that's ok, but you will find great benefit from bringing your values and goals into deeper alignment.

Q: In which 3 ways do you spend your money?

_____

_____

_____

5) Where do you have the most order and organization?
Often, we find that the things that are the most important to us we keep well-organized, whereas things that are low on our value scale often fall into a state of disarray. So if you take a look at the areas of your life and things in your life that are the most well-organized, you can get a good glimpse into what things matter most to you.

Q: In which 3 areas are you most organized?

_____

_____

_____

6) Where are you most reliable, disciplined, and focused?
Seldom do we need to be reminded by someone else to do the things that we value the most. You naturally know and appreciate that these things just need to be done, and so you get them done. You are internally motivated to do them because they matter to you. Look at the things you do, the ways you spend your time, and your goals that you are disciplined, reliable, and focused about—the things you feel naturally self-motivated to do.

Q: In which 3 activities are you the most disciplined, focused, and reliable?

_____

_____

_____

7) What do you think about most often?
What is your most dominant thought? We're not talking about the negative self-thoughts or the things that distract you. We're not talking about the fantasies, "shoulds", or "ought to's". I want you to examine, to find out what you envision or desire for how you want your life to be. Focus on the thoughts that you show some progress towards obtaining, no matter how slow and steady.

Q: What are your 3 most dominant thoughts in this area?

_____

_____

8) What is your internal dialogue?

What things do you find yourself saying to yourself the most, things that can actually help you get towards where you want to go? I am not talking about the negative self-talk we all do, like "I'll never get this done in time" or "I feel so out of shape". Think of what you really desire, no matter how far away you think it may be, and what things you say to yourself that actually seem to be coming true and at least bearing some fruit.

Q: What are 3 things that you have internal dialogues about?

_____

_____

_____

9) What do you talk about in social settings?

When you are out with others, what things do you find yourself wanting to bring up and talk about? What things are you excited to share with others? What things don't you want to talk about? What subjects turn you into an instant introvert (someone very shy) or extrovert (someone who is very outgoing)? Whether you are by nature an introvert or an extrovert, there are probably some topics that immediately bring you to life and get you started talking, and others that immediately shut you down and you have nothing to say.

You can also use these observations to help see other people's values. For example, if you are speaking with someone and the first thing they do is to ask how your kids are, it likely suggests kids are of value to them. If they ask you about work or business, or if you are seeing someone new, these can very well be things they are placing value on. Topics that you feel drawn to, or things that you feel like sharing your thoughts on are often a key to discovering what you value.

Q: What are the top 3 things you talk about while with others?

_____

_____

_____

10) What inspires you?
Ask yourself what excites you? What motivates you? What inspires you now? What has inspired you in the past? Who inspires you? What is common to the people who inspire you? Take your time with this part, because figuring out what excites/motivates/inspires you is very powerful in revealing what you value most!

Q: What are the 3 things that inspire you the most?

_____

_____

_____

11) What are the most consistent long-term goals that you have set?
What are the three top long-term goals that you have set that you are slowly but surely actually making happen? Don't write down fantasies that you are not doing anything about, look at

the dreams that you think about, that dominate your mind, that perhaps each day you are bringing into your life, step by step.

Q: What are the three most consistent long-term goals that you have set?

_____

_____

_____

12) What do you love to learn/read/absorb information about the most?

What are the three most common topics you love learning about the most? Maybe you read books on topics can you stay focused on the longest without distraction? What subjects can you get lost in thinking about?

Q: What are the 3 things you love to learn about and that you can spend your focus on?

_____

_____

_____

Crystallize your values

OK, here is the payoff! This is where we pull together all the work you have just done, all the introspection ... and help you find your top values, what is most important to you ... and what you should ensure you are including as part of your life!

Looking at your answers, you will see some repetition among the 36 answers and a lot of answers that are quite similar. You may find that you are expressing the same kinds of values, but in different ways. An example might be "spending time with people I like", "having a drink with the folks at work", going out to eat with my friends"; they may seem like different answers, but if you look closer, you will see patterns that emerge.

So look at the answer that is repeated the most often, and write down how many times it was repeated (i.e. spending time with friends - 4). Then find the second most frequent answer and write down that number, then find the third and fourth, and so on, until you have ranked every answer.

This exercise should give you some good insights into yourself; it should give you an indicator of what your values are, what makes you tick. Are you surprised? I find that for many people although they may be a little surprised to see it actually written down on paper, they can *feel* that it aligns with their inner self. They have a *sense* that it is right. Even if they had never thought about it as such, it makes sense at a deeper level.

And guess what? You are now communicating with your inner Warrior! The Warrior within you is alive!

> **TO DO:**
> 1) Review the top 3 answers you identified and really look to see whether these things currently play a major role in your life, in your day-to-day activities. If they currently are, are they represented enough? Realize that if your top values, if the things that really make your heart soar, are not a big enough part of your life, then of course your life will be out of balance!
>
> 2) Make a list of ways that you can add these things into your life more.

Incorporating these values into your life

To awaken your Warrior within, you need to start incorporating the top answers into your life, because they directly connect to your passion and purpose. You need to make sure that your number one answer is included in your life! This is critical to feeling fully alive again, and having the energy, zest, passion, and self-confidence you want!

You can now start to make decisions about life, and in the everyday battles of life, based on your hierarchy of values. For many people, you will have valid and empowering proof of how your life is already demonstrating your commitment to your values. We will look at this more in depth later, but here is something to think about career-wise: just because Aunt Sandra hooked you up with a cushy job, that doesn't necessarily mean that is the job you should be doing in life.

Life is too short to not do things that make you feel alive! We have to value every day as if it is precious. We have to live every day as if it could be our last day on earth. We cannot afford to let the hand on the clock just keep ticking and ticking without really living. It is so important that you start to really believe this, and to start working on it. It is time to start breaking through what you thought was your comfort zone, and build a newly expanded one! Remember, if you do what is hard right now, then life becomes easy; if you do what is easy, then life becomes hard.

"Doing something you hate is not a living, it is a dying" - **Mark A.**

How to make space in your life for your passion and purpose

Now that you have identified things that are very important to you, and you know they should be included in your day-to-day activities, you need a clear strategy to achieve this. One of the things that holds people back from adding things into their life that energize them is that they are too busy doing things that *don't* energize them. In many cases, people find that they are doing things in life that actually suck the life and energy from them!

> Realize that if your passion and purpose are not a big enough part of your life, then your life will be out of alignment! If you are spending every day doing things that <u>are not</u> important to you, to your inner self, to your soul, then how can you feel fully alive? Your energy, your Warrior's energy, depends on aligning your life with your heart.

If you really look at the concept of things that energize you (make your feel alive and happy) vs. things that de-energize you (things that make you tired, lethargic, or depressed), there are certain areas that will stand out:

- **People** - There are people who energize you. These are people that you love to spend time with. There are also people that actually drain you. When you finish spending time with them, you feel tired, spent, and less than inspired.

> **TO DO:**
> Make a list of people that energize you and find ways to spend more time with them. Also make a list of people who take your energy from you, and either find a way to change your relationship, or consider reducing/eliminating your time spent with them.

- **Places** - There are places that fill you with energy. For many people, an art gallery or a beautiful lake may fill them with great feelings. There are also places that just suck the energy from you. For many people, crowded cities with no greenery exhaust them, and the mall at Christmas time is a place they try at all costs to avoid. Each of us will have places that inspire and energize, and places that drain and uninspired us.

> **TO DO:**
> Make a list of the places that give you energy and the places that take your energy. Plan a strategy to avoid the places that take your energy and increase the time you spend in the places that make you feel great!

- **Times of the day** - Some people find themselves most productive waking up at 5 a.m., while others do their best work late at night, even turning out their light at 5 a.m.

> **TO DO:**
> Find the times you are most inefficient and the times you feel your best. Look at scheduling your day this way. It may take a little bit of experimentation.

- **Activities** - As we discussed earlier, there are certain things, or types of things, we do that energize us, and actually give us more energy. There are also other things we do that we dread thinking of, that immediately make us tired, and where time crawls while we're doing them.

Removing energy drainers

To ensure that you have your life set up in a way that you can truly live your passion and purpose, you first need to start eliminating things from your life that suck up your energy—that take energy from you. This will open up a space in your life, a sort of void. Then you need to insert the things that add energy to you. So we will create an opening in your life by subtracting things that are taking your energy and holding you back, and then fill the space by inserting things that can move you forward. This is not necessarily as easy as it sounds, but is **critical** to fully awakening your Warrior within!

Let's say that there were certain people that you feel are always negative, who always complain. You meet up with them feeling great, but by the time you leave them, you just want to crawl into bed and sleep. You may find yourself dreading spending time with them. You may decide that either your interactions needed to change, or else you have to decrease or eliminate your time with them.

There are likely times during the day when you feel more focused and productive, and times when you feel less effective. Many people feel tired around 3 p.m., or if they eat a big meal.

If you look at the activities that wear you out, you might be surprised to find that you waste a lot of your time doing activities that you don't enjoy, that take energy from you, that you don't really need to be doing personally, or that could be eliminated from your life altogether *and* not be missed one bit.

Delegation and elimination

So there may be some things in your life that need to be done as they are important, but not necessarily by you. For example, if you are struggling with bookkeeping and tax preparation, you can hire someone to do it for you; it may cost a little bit more, but it may save you dreading it. It also saves you spending all that energy on something you don't like and that doesn't need to be done by you personally. Instead, you can now invest that energy into something you enjoy and something that can move you forward in life.

You could also delegate by bartering (or swapping skills). Perhaps you love doing websites or keeping social media things up dated, but you dread cutting your lawn. What if there was someone in your area who ran a business, but was very uncomfortable with computers? What if they dreaded having to think about the upkeep of their small business website, or keeping their Facebook page up to date, but they absolutely loved to spend time outside doing yard work? How powerful would it be if you could swap something you hated doing for something you loved doing, and not lose out at all? How much *more* energy would you have in life? One way to find someone like this is to look for people advertising the services you want to get in your local paper and give them a call. The worse thing that could happen is they say they are not interested ... but they might actually say yes, or know someone who would be interested.

Finally, there are things you do in life that you could just totally eliminate and not even notice. Do you ever find yourself getting distracted at the computer when you sit down to do some work? What if every time you sit down at your computer, you take just 10 minutes to quickly look at all the news sites, just to see what's going on in the world? A big problem is that the news is always negative, and the negative will instantly zap some of your positive energy that you had ready for your task.

What if you did this just 6 times a day? That equals 60 minutes of time not only totally wasted, but 60 minutes that sucked the positive energy out of you. The answer: just stop doing it (or at the very least, cut down the amount you watch). Will you miss it? Well, at first you will probably find yourself thinking "I hope I am not missing out on any hugely important news event" (even though so many "news" items cover things like "What are the people in Hollywood wearing lately?"). But you are most likely apt to soon find out you missed nothing, and in fact feel mentally and physically better, and are much more productive!

> What things in your life can you eliminate by delegating to someone else, by trading services, or by simply eliminating them? And more importantly, what things in your life can you then add that will energize your Warrior within?   **?**

What <u>feels</u> right to you?

Another tool you can use to decide whether something is your passion or your purpose is to allow yourself to **feel** it. Remember, a real Warrior will look deep into their **self** to find out what makes them tick, what they are about, what they stand for. To do this, they need to listen to themselves, to be *in tune* with their body, mind, and spirit. They need to block out all the outside noise; I often use this technique when deciding whether I should do something.

> Think about it, you have most likely used this technique before. Have you ever had an instance where you have thought of doing something, but something about it just didn't feel quite right? Perhaps it gave you a knot in your stomach, or you felt yourself holding your breath in a nervous manner. Maybe after thinking about it, you started to develop a mild headache. Perhaps you were restless at night and couldn't sleep well. These are all indications that you knew whatever you were thinking about was incompatible with your inner Warrior!
>
> Now think of a time when you were trying to decide on something and it just felt right! Maybe a wave of calmness or certainty swept over you? Perhaps you felt a joyousness sweep over you? Maybe you just broke out into a big smile? And you *knew* that it felt right.
>
> That is your intuition speaking to you. It is your Warrior within speaking to you. You need to start to listen to yourself!

Every Warrior needs a mission

Think back to almost every Warrior story you have ever read or seen—the main thing they all have in common is that the hero must embark on a journey or on a mission to find themselves, to prove themselves.

The usual ingredients to a good hero story are:
1. **The Hero Gets Called To an Adventure** - A hero is given a message, often in a mysterious way. In my case, the message was given to me by my body, or at least it tried to give it to me. It kept breaking down and getting sick. It brought me into periods of depression and apathy. It was trying to tell me I had do go on a mission to change my life. What is calling you to start your journey?

2. **The Hero Initially Refuses The Call** – Often, the hero will turn down the mission at first, and not take that chance at adventure. I know that I was refusing it, when I choose to keep ignoring the signs that I was totally crashing, when I continued to isolate myself in a type of self-imposed darkness, I was turning down the opportunity to go on the mission (at least at first). What is holding you back from beginning your adventure?
3. **The Hero Meets A Mentor** - The hero will gain help from someone wiser and more experienced who will aid them. By educating myself and listening to mentors, I gained the courage to begin my journey. This book, our connection, can be the thing that will finally help you take the action you need to take.
4. **The Hero Encounters Many Challenges** - The hero will have many challenges. These usually include escaping a place in which they are imprisoned. I was imprisoned by my lack of energy, by my lack of motivation, by allowing myself to be trapped in a tiny little box mentally, which seemed hard to burst free from. You will face trials and tribulations, things that will test you, but know in your heart that everything you need to succeed is within you; you just need to bring it out!
5. **The Hero Eventually Earns The Ultimate Reward** - With perseverance, the hero is finally able to defeat his enemies, and the hero is rewarded with new knowledge or power or ability. I fought hard to break free and take control of my life again! I was rewarded with renewed energy and passion, with a clear purpose in life and happiness. You too can transform yourself and live the life of your dreams. You were meant to!

Your Warrior needs to go on a quest

One day, I came across a book by Chris Guillebeau called "*The Happiness of Pursuit*", a collection of stories about various people around the world who went on quests. Over the years, the author had actually visited every single country in the world. It became a mission for him, a journey to go on, and it was something that helped add meaning to his life.

I thought to myself, how amazing would it be to go on a journey, on a quest? All of a sudden I could feel my heart start to beat faster, and a smile came to my face. It was exactly what I needed. Of late, I had been starting to feel a little complacent. I had been starting to watch TV more, I hadn't exercised much lately, and I was starting to eat more junk food. These are all red flags for me that I need to catch myself and get back on track.

> **TO DO:**
> If you haven't already done it, watch the movie I mentioned in the introduction, *The Secret Life of Walter Mitty* to see Walter's inspirational quest.

I went home and talked to my wife about it. We came up with the plan that we would go for a 4-day hike on the Bruce Trail (a trail that winds in total 885 km in total through Ontario.) It was quite exciting because neither of us had done something that would require so much stamina for many years. We decided we could afford to take 4 days off work and started to map out a 4-day hike. We looked things up on the internet, searching for tips from anyone that had gone before us. We went to the store and bought supplies like trail mix, mosquito nets, bug spray, and a tiny but powerful flashlight. We borrowed knapsacks, got our camelbacks cleaned out for water. We looked at the weather forecast, and arranged where we would sleep each night. We were ready!

We completed our hike with an amazing feeling of accomplishment and pride. It was so much tougher than we had anticipated. I had calculated we would need to hike for 8 hours a day to reach our stopovers for the night, but it actually took us close to 11 hours each day of hiking. The paths led us up and down, and up and down, the escarpments. The first day, I ran out of water 3 hours before the finish, and my muscles began to cramp up severely from dehydration. The mosquitoes were unrelenting in sections, and we actually almost sprinted out of some the denser parts of the woods to get some relief from them.

It was challenging, but it was awesome! During those 4 days of hiking, I felt as alive as I have ever felt.

That is the power of a journey or quest. Leading up to the adventure gives you something to look forward to, something to plan for, and that in its self can kick-start your mind! And the journey itself could reward you with so many unforeseen challenges and wonders, so many opportunities to learn about yourself and the world. It can revitalize you physically, emotionally, mentally, and spiritually. This is the awakening your Warrior within is craving!

Personally, I emerged from my journey a subtly changed person. I realized I could survive a day without my phone on, checking emails every five minutes. I discovered that I missed nature and needed to somehow make it a bigger part of my life.
At fifty years old, I realized that I was not done, that I had so much more left in me. That my body did have limitations, but they didn't have to stop me from exploring and living. That I was mentally stronger than I had realized, that pushing through

those days of fatigue and pain and heat and bugs, no matter how slowly I'd had to go at times, that I did it! I finished it, even if I didn't do it as quickly as a twenty-year-old me would have done.

> What mission do you want to go on? What excites you and gets your blood flowing? You can start planning a big mission because that is mentally very invigorating. However, I strongly suggest that you pick a small mission, one that you can do right away... and then just do it! This will spark your Warrior within at the deepest level! **?**

CHAPTER 3: Strengthening Your Warrior's Mind

"The mind is everything. What you think you become." - **Buddha**
"The energy of the mind is the essence of life." - **Aristotle**

Your thoughts create everything that you are.

You manifest, or bring forth, everything in your life with your thoughts, both good and bad. Your mind and what you think about are the single most important things in your life. And it is an area that, for the most part, we as a society totally ignore. This is one of the major reasons our society is in such a bad way. The great thing is that you have the absolute power to change it when you mentally strengthen your Warrior within.

Just as it is important that we strengthen our physical bodies with nutritious and energizing food, it is important to fuel our minds with healthy, awakening food. If we fill our bodies with crap, it will detract from the performance of our bodies, fill them with sludge, and make it easier for them to break down.

The same is true for our minds. What we listen to, read, and watch is food for our minds. What we think about has tremendous power over our health.

So in this chapter, the question I ask you is "What are you feeding your mind?"
- What are you reading and watching?
- What are you filling your mind with?
- What do you spend your time thinking about?
- Are you thinking self-defeating thoughts
- How do you change your mindset?

How do you start your day?

On any morning, if you wake up and check the news first thing, you could be greeted with murder, wars, kidnappings, and more. Just a few minutes of this negativity can cause your body to react negatively too, such as having a tight feeling in your chest, having shallow breathing, a mild headache, and feeling uneasy. The things that you ingest into your mind can completely transform yourself mentally and physically in under 5 minutes!

This is an example of the power and importance of what you fill your mind with. This is just a few minutes. The fact is we are bombarded with negativity 24/7 ... via social media, newspapers, internet sites, television ... there are even monitors in malls now, in airports, at the gym ... unless you wear blinders, it almost seems impossible to escape it! Imagine what builds up inside of your body and your mind if you experience this for just one full day. Imagine if you experience it every day for a week? Imagine if you experience it literally every day of your life. It is *no* wonder then that your Warrior within enters such a state you don't even know it is there.

If you find yourself checking the news first thing and feeling anxious, an immediate solution is to close your computer browsers, put on some nice music, and do some Qi Gong exercises for five minutes (this will be covered in the *Energizing Your Warrior Within* section). Take 5 minutes to completely reverse all of this negativity. This is one example of how you awaken your own Warrior, and more importantly how you keep your Warrior strong and healthy once awakened.

> **TO DO:**
> What things do you watch on TV, or read, or view on the web? Write down beside each one whether they are helping you or hindering you. Are they filling your mind with good food, or clogging it with useless negativity?

Are you thinking self-defeating thoughts?

We have enough outside forces trying to hold us down at times, so the last thing we need is to be our own worst enemy. But that is exactly what we do when we allow ourselves to play the "woe is me" game. We tell ourselves: *I am fat. I am out of shape. I am not smart enough. I am not good looking enough. I wish I had that guys six pack abs (but I know that will never happen). I suck. I will never win. I am a loser.*

This is pure self-sabotage. If you allow yourself to *dwell* on these negative things, you run the risk of poisoning your entire being: mentally, physically, and spiritually.

Let's face it, everyone is going to have self-doubt flash into their minds from time to time. Those that accept it and give in are destined to walk around with a gloomy look on their face, and fear and lack of confidence gnawing at their gut. This leads to your Warrior within falling down. A healthy Warrior does not accept this type of thinking. To heal your Warrior, you must become aware of what is going on in your own mind and make any changes that are necessary. You need to consciously monitor what you are thinking, and ensure that your own mind is not taking you down a slippery slope.

For many people, the self-limiting thoughts that bounce about in their heads are their worst enemies. They are killers, because the person may not even be aware that they have these thoughts, and yet it is these "secret" limiting thoughts that continually hold them back from achieving their dreams. Every time they draw close to an amazing accomplishment, that limiting belief pops into their head without their knowledge and sabotages it.

So you need to identify what thoughts or fears hold you back and work on them. Nothing will change until you change. Your mindset brought you here, so for you to change, you must change your mindset.

What fears are holding you back from success, from being happy? Are they rational? In what ways can you overcome each of these fears? For example, if you have a fear of public speaking, you could take a course on public speaking, increase your vocabulary, practice voice projection, join a speech making group, start making small presentations at work or to your family, record yourself speaking, and drink more water to keep yourself properly hydrated so that your mouth doesn't get dry.

> **TO DO:**
> What are the self-sabotaging things you say to yourself? Write them down. Then beside them write down the opposites. These opposites are very powerful. They are what you want to become, or be viewed as.

How do you rewire your mind and change your thinking?

Instead of allowing yourself to think negative, self-limiting thoughts about yourself, you need to rewire your mind by filling it with empowering thoughts!

> Many times, when people think they need to make a change in their lives, they change only their actions ... and that is a good start. But what you really need to do is change your thinking as well! Change your thinking, change your life. Change your thoughts, change your life.

If you find yourself feeling very low, one solution to improve your mood is to use positive and empowering affirmations. Life Success Coach Tony Robbins suggests some simple but powerful affirmations such as "Every day, in every way, I'm getting stronger and stronger", and "Every day, in every way, I'm getting better and better".

You can say this positive self-talk quietly to yourself, or even just in your mind, and it will help. But it is even more powerful to say them out loud! At first, you might feel a little silly, but try it—it will work. If you really want these ideas to resonate with you, then shout them out loud! Then add motion ... walk around your room so you your physical energy is moving, then shout out your empowering affirmations. Then finally, to make them even more powerful, do this with a huge smile on your face!

You can make up your own affirmations for whatever you want. You can write them to promote your good health, your success in business, that you appreciate things, or that you are a confident and positive person. The very act of writing these out feels very empowering, and reading them silently is helpful, but speaking them out loud has that much more impact.

> **TO DO:**
> Write down 5-10 positive affirmations that you can say to yourself every day. When you say them, say them out loud and with feeling and passion.

"You want to become aware of your thoughts and choose your thoughts carefully and you want to have fun with this, because you are the masterpiece of your own life. You are the Michelangelo of your own life. The David you are sculpting is you." – **Dr. Joe Vitale**

Alter your thoughts subconsciously

I use a very power software system that actually rewires my mind subconsciously. Subliminal messages are positive affirmations sent *directly* to the subconscious mind, bypassing the more critical thinking conscious mind. The subconscious then follows these commands to produce **powerful** and **exciting** positive stimulation. **Prosperity Power**™ subliminal programming software works by flashing positive affirmations around your computer screen while you work. The messages are completely unobtrusive. In fact, you probably won't even notice most of them. But the subconscious does. It soaks up every single message—customized to your desires. In the near future, I will make this available to those that are interested.

Where focus goes, energy flows

Your mind has great power over what you do in life. The expression "Where focus goes, energy flows" is a very deep and accurate concept. I want you to think about this, and what it means. If you are thinking about eating a hot fudge sundae, even if you don't have the ingredients in your house, if you think about it long and hard enough, you may find yourself driving over to your local ice cream place to get one.

This concept is used a lot in sports such golf. For example, a player is having trouble putting (the finesse part of putting the ball in the hole). They find themselves dreading putting their ball on the green because they are afraid they will miss their next putt, even if it is normally an easy one. All the putting practice in the world won't matter if their mind is convinced they are going to miss, because that limiting belief will find a way to sabotage their next shot.

But what if they changed their thinking from fear of missing (sending all their energy to missing), to envisioning themselves executing all the basics of the putting stroke perfectly (which is 100% within their control), and then in their mind seeing the ball glide perfectly toward the hole and then drop in (sending all their energy to a made putt)?

This technique works dramatically well for many players. Many athletes actually go through their whole event mentally first (a gymnastics routine, an Olympic ski run). They see themselves make every move, every shot, perfectly in their mind before they ever set out on the gym floor or the ski slope.

So try picturing your next work presentation in its entirety in your mind before you ever give it! Envision where you will stand, see yourself flicking through the PowerPoint slides, picture the people you are presenting to, see them smiling with admiration for all the work you had put in, feel their applause raining down on you at the completion of your presentation, people coming up to you and slapping you on the back and giving you high fives? Picture how great you feel that you pulled it off, how proud you are. Then take that feeling into your actual presentation. This will make a difference compared to lying awake all night worrying that you will screw up.

The concept of positive energy is explored in *"The Secret"* by Rhonda Byrne, a book and movie about a concept called the law of attraction. The idea is that you will attract the same type of energy that you put out into the world. Or another way to say it is that *you get what you think about*. If you put out negative energy, you will attract negative things. If you put out positive energy, you will attract positive things.

> Remember, whatever you think about is where your energy tends to go towards accomplishing it, whether you are aware of it or not. *Positive energy leads to positive results.*

When we are first taught to drive, we are taught something that seems at first somewhat contradictory. When we are going around a corner, we are taught not to look right in front of us, but to look further up the curve. As I was first learning to drive around a corner I was a little nervous, and so I kept looking right over my hood at the road below. But if you think about it, on that curve, it you look right ahead of you, you are actually looking *off* the road, and if you allowed the car to follow where your eyes were leading it, you would drive right off the curve. However if you can train yourself to look further ahead, up the curve, your car will naturally follow and navigate the curve successfully.

The same thing is so true in life. You need to focus on what you **do** want, not on what you don't want. *Where do you want to go?*

> Are you thinking about what you *want* or what you *don't want*? Are you thinking about what you want to happen or what you don't want to happen? Are you thinking about where you want to go, or where you don't want to go? **?**

Let's say you are trying to lose some weight. You find yourself in the local coffee place. You say to yourself "Do **not** eat that donut". Pretty simple right? Maybe you back it up with "That donut will wreck my diet. That donut will make me fat. Gotta stay away from the donut even though it would taste so good." However, what does your mind actually focus on? It hears DONUT! And guess what happens? You eat it.

What if at the coffee shop, you just said to yourself "I always make healthy eating decisions"?

Start really examining how you phrase things. If you have never tried this, you need to experiment with it right away. It is extremely powerful. The mind programming software I discussed earlier can really help this.

"Here's the problem. Most people are thinking about what they don't want and they're wondering why it shows up over and over again." – **John Assaraf**

Don't allow yourself to play the victim card

You might believe that life has been unfair to you. That some mysterious force accounts for your bad fate. And since it is some mysterious thing out there, you believe that you have **no** control over it.

The concept of control is very important when it comes to being a victim. If you blame bad things on an external factor, it is obviously beyond your control, and so you feel **powerless**. It is so important for us to take personal responsibility.

I had to learn this lesson personally. It is true that I was younger than most people who had heart complications. However, what I wasn't acknowledging was that I partly put myself in that position. I was the one who made the decision to have an out of balance life. I worked longer hours than I had to, I ate crappy food, and I didn't exercise. *I did those things*. *I did have control over those things*. Those decisions *I made* are the main things that led to my body wearing down. If I had acknowledged that, then my problems would have been internally created, and if I created them, then I had the power to fix them! If I had realized this, then I could have avoided feeling so angry for so many years.

> What things in life have you been blaming on anyone else but yourself? Can you see how by taking some personal responsibility for it happening, it actually gives you the power to now change it? **?**

Fight or flight

The fact is that we have all had bad things happen to us. The world has been unfair to all of us, and for some people horrific things have happened, things I cannot even imagine. But we cannot let that define who we are, how we view things, and how we act. Anger is an emotion that *will* give your inner Warrior instant energy. Of course, there are times when it is necessary to get that energy surge, to get that fight or flight reaction. It can get you out of trouble; it could save your life. **However**, you need to learn how to turn it off.

Inside your body, there are things called adrenal glands, which sit on top of each of your kidneys. When your body experiences some kind of stressful situation and need a surge of energy, they kick out adrenalin into your blood stream. Let's say you are walking alone at night in a parking lot, and all of a sudden you hear a "clink" from somewhere. Immediately, your adrenalin kicks in. Your sympathetic nervous system is activated. It raises your heart rate, getting your heart beating faster, which pumps out more blood into your body so that your muscles have the blood and energy they need to run or fight if you need to. Your blood vessels constrict, increasing your blood pressure. Your breathing becomes faster and shallower. You are suddenly more alert. Your pupils dilate. Your senses are heightened, and your sense of smell, hearing, and vision are all more acute.

But by drawing energy to some parts of your body, it also takes energy away from others areas of your body, such as slowing down your digestion system (which can cause constipation or diarrhea), decreasing your sexual arousal, and limiting your saliva production. Our ancestors needed adrenalin to kick into fight or flight mode because if they were suddenly approached by a wild animal, it could save their life. Warriors needed this reaction on the battlefield.

But when the danger subsides, and the stressful situation is over, things go back to normal, the sympathetic nervous system shuts down, and the parasympathetic nervous system takes over. While the sympathetic nervous system is nicknamed the "fight or flight" system, the parasympathetic nervous system is nicknamed the "rest and digest" system. So your heart rate will decrease, you can start to take some nice deep breaths again, and your digestive system can return to its normal functioning. The "rest and digest" system allows your body to **recover**.

If you stay in a constant state of fight or flight, you never allow your body to recover, to rejuvenate. As I look back, I ran on this fight or flight for the most part for years on end. My adrenal glands became fatigued and unable to function at full force. Imagine taking away the secret weapon of your Warrior! It becomes powerless and unable to function properly.

Left unchecked, stress can have many more debilitating effects on your body. It can lead to:

- Digestion problems, causing things such as diarrhea, constipation, and acid reflux
- High blood pressure (which causes your heart to work harder to pump blood), and could potentially lead to heart attacks and strokes
- Anxiety and depression
- Obesity
- Sleep problems
- And many more issues

You need to turn it down and allow it to rest, to reduce the stress and strain you are putting on it. You need to be aware of this sort of thing, because you don't want this to happen to yourself, and if it is already happening to you, you need to be able to fix it.

What causes the fight or flight system to kick in?

The fight or flight response is caused by things that your mind perceives are potential threats to you. Anger. Fear. Stress. Surprise. It doesn't matter whether you are afraid of something that is a real threat or just an imaginary, perceived one. You mind may not be able to tell the difference and so it will send out defensive commands to the body nonetheless.

The important thing is that you need to be able to turn it off and allow your body to rest.

There are so many ways of telling your body and mind to relax. Qi Gong, Tai Chi, Yoga, meditation, walking, calming music ... anything where you can allow yourself to relax mentally and give your body a chance to rejuvenate. One of the ways is deep breathing (breathing from your diaphragm as opposed to your upper chest), and it is so helpful because when you take a deep breath into your belly and really cause your diaphragm to expand, it slows your heart rate down, which makes you less anxious, and it helps your adrenal glands to reset.

> Do you find yourself getting caught in a state of fight or flight? What things, events, or conditions cause you to get into this state? Can you release them immediately or do they dwell in your mind? If so, what are some things you can do to put your mind and body back into a more relaxed state so they can rejuvenate themselves?

Change your state

When you are feeling down, or sad, or angry, one of the biggest favors you can do for yourself is to promptly change your mental state. The quicker you can do it generally, the better. That is why it is important to really get to know yourself, to listen to your self, to be in tune with yourself. If you find you are sliding too quickly or too easily into a mental state that is not helpful for you, then you need to mentally and energetically shake yourself!

For example, if driving in heavy traffic puts you in an irritated mood, then do something to change your mental state. Open your window to get some fresh air. Turn on some "happy" or "relaxing" music. Think about something you are looking forward to. Smile.

Some easy ways to change your state are:
- Sing
- Smile
- Clap your hands
- Dance
- Go for a walk
- Spend some time in nature
- Give your pet some snuggles
- Hug your family
- Eat something really nutritious and light
- Put on happy music
- Read something motivating or inspirational

> **TO DO:**
> Write down your top 3 things you could do to instantly change your state of mind to one of positivity.

Do something that will **jolt** you out of your the current state you want to get out of. Now we'll talk about some ways you can change your mental state.

Laughter

"Always laugh when you can ... it is a cheap medicine." - **Lord Byron**

Laughter is amazing medicine for the soul. Laughter helps lift the spirits of your Warrior within. We should all make sure we laugh, a deep belly laugh, a laugh that makes tears run down our face! American political journalist Norman Cousins helped heal himself of a serious condition, and he describes his journey in his book *"Anatomy of an Illness"*. He says he would watch funny movies each day and make himself laugh, and he believes it helped extend his life well past what the doctors might have thought.

Laughter may help you to:
- Improve your overall attitude
- Reduce stress/tension
- Promote relaxation
- Improve your sleep
- Enhance your quality of life
- Strengthen your social bonds and relationships
- Produce a general sense of wellbeing

So next time you go to the movies, look for one that will make you laugh. If you are on Netflix or some internet movie site, search in the comedy section.

> Make a commitment with yourself to laugh more! Read, listen to, and watch things that make you laugh. Look back at happy and funny events in your life with a loved one and reminisce and laugh!

Get organized

When you allow yourself to not care about the little things, like staying generally organized for example, that it is one of the things that starts to sap energy from your Warrior within. So when you take the time to start focusing on the little details, it helps give your Warrior that extra push up.

If you find you are out of whack, you can do little things to get yourself back on track. Tidy up your work area at work. Get some cleaner and wipe down the dashboard of your car ... if you are feeling particularly adventurous, visit a car cleaning center and give it a quick vacuum and wash. Get your hair trimmed. Take 10 minutes and clean off your bedside table—you'll be amazed how this one little difference can send a jolt of happiness and freshness through you mind.

Make your lunch the night before! Prep something nutritious that will feed your body, store it, put it in the fridge. When you wake up the next morning, you don't have to worry about a thing, just grab your lunch as you head out the door. Plus it has the added bonus of allowing your body to feel great and not get the mid-afternoon feeling of being bogged down and tired when you eat fast food or junk food!

> **TO DO:**
> Pick a little area that you want to clean up and get organized. Ensure you make it just a small area, so that you don't feel overwhelmed, which could prevent you from doing it. Take a before picture, then just do it, and take a picture after. Send it to me and I can stick it up on my website to inspire others. Importantly, have fun!

Gratitude and appreciation

One of the most powerful feelings that you can have—something that can instantly transform your feelings to a higher level—is when you focus on the things you are thankful for. Remember that where focus goes, energy flows. At times, you will find your mind focusing on what you don't have, or wishing you had, instead of rejoicing in what you do have. Even though we may have some down days, you can rest assured that someone, somewhere in the world is having a much worse day than you. You might be frustrated that your car overheated and you are stuck on the side of a highway. But for certain, there are many people who would give anything to have a car, to even have the chance to have it break down.

When you are in a state of gratitude, there is no room left for things life anger, sadness, or depression. It is that **powerful**!

There are so many things you could be thankful for:
- Your health
- Your family
- The air you breathe
- The food you eat
- The birds in the sky
- Your favorite song
- The sunshine
- The moonlight
- The grass beneath your feet
- … And so much more!

> **Feel the power of gratitude right now.** Write down a list of things you are thankful for, no matter how big or small, and add to it every day as you think of new things. Look at this list every day, think about it, and let it soak into your mind. The feelings this will elicit can smooth over any sadness, and you won't be able to help smiling.
>
> Realize how very lucky you are. To be alive. To be able to experience the world, even the downs, because they made the ups feel even that much better. A very empowering exercise to show gratitude, and to make someone's day is to give a handwritten note to someone who does something you are very appreciative for (such as superb service at a restaurant).

Forgive yourself and don't set unrealistic expectations for yourself

We are too hard on ourselves. We often expect ourselves to be perfect. We beat ourselves up for things that we consider failures, and even over things we actually have no control over.

We are often harder on ourselves than even our worst critics are. And what good does that do?

People tell me that it is important that we hold ourselves to high standards, and I can agree with that. However, first, they have to be standards that we have a chance to uphold. For example, let's say you had golfed earlier in your life, but hadn't done so for many years. If you were to suddenly take up golf again and went out playing with friends who have golfed every day for the past 10 years, you would have to be fair with yourself.

"I forgive myself and set myself free" - **Louise Hay**

Each swing they take is smooth and effortless, their shots all land in the middle of the fairway or middle of the green. When you swing, it is crooked, the ball hooks and ends up in the woods. When you are really down, you might get angry at yourself. You think to yourself, "How could I not be as good as my friends?" But the answer is very simple: there is really no way you could have been given your lack of playing. It is **unfair** to yourself to expect yourself to play as well as them. You need to learn to forgive yourself for each bad shot. You need to just play within your own means, and be happy with that. Could you get better over time? Yes ... but with time.

Set the rules of the game so that you can win.

"The weak can never forgive, forgiveness is the attribute of the strong" - **Mahatma Ghandi**

Meditation

Meditation is a very powerful tool, yet many people struggle with the concept of meditation. It is taught by so many people, in so many different ways. For some reason, people believe that the goal of meditation is to put your mind in such a place where it thinks of nothing. And despite their best efforts, some thought about something would wander into their mind and they would feel that they *failed* at meditation. It can get to the point where they begin to not even want to think about meditating because they don't feel they could succeed at it. And that is the absolute opposite of what meditation is about.

Meditation can be a huge tool for you, but you need to view mediation within a different framework. View it as just a state of mindfulness, of being here and now. Of not worrying about the future. Of enjoying what is happening now. And it is not easy necessarily. You have likely seen people who it seems like their head is always somewhere else. You may be talking to them, and they may be responding, but it doesn't really seem like their attention is with you in that moment—they are somewhere far away.

This is something you must try to remind yourself of constantly. For example, you may be talking to someone, but part of your mind is thinking about a big event coming up, and what you need to finish for it. Try to quiet your mind, to calm it down, and to focus on just one thing ... what is happening right now in this moment in time, in this location you are standing. You will find it quite a relaxing experience. It forces you to stop trying to focus on three things, and not really listening to any of them, and instead to just fully focusing on one. It is so much more satisfying.

Perhaps you are a master of mediation and you can teach me the way. But if you are not, then that the very act of simply trying to calm and focus your mind on the here and now—of trying to be more centered—will be a very empowering action that can pay big rewards for you and your Warrior within on your mission of happiness!

> Are you able to always stay in the here and now or do you find yourself drifting? If so, practice being aware of where you are, and trying to bring yourself back to be fully present wherever you are.

Challenge yourself

One of the very important ways to keep your Warrior within healthy is to challenge yourself from time to time, mentally and physically. Complacency is a poison that seeps into your body and mind, and is one of the things that leads to your Warrior sliding down. We all need to be challenged. It keeps us growing. It keeps us learning new things. It keeps us moving. Challenging yourself mentally or physically or spiritually helps you find out what you're made of, and may constantly surprise you as you realize you are more and more powerful than you imagined. Your spirit wants to be challenged—it wants to grow—it wants to evolve.

Go on a long bike ride. Hike a trail and camp along the way. Take some courses to learn something new that you are passionate about. Try a karate class. Start that part-time business you have been thinking about in the back of your mind. Sing at a Karaoke bar. Do something that is a little out of your everyday routine. It is ok to be a little nervous about it. You are built of more than you know.

Of course, ensure you are safe about it! Always make sure you are prepared and that you have a friend with you or someone who knows what they are doing. But the key is that we all need to **step out of our comfort zone** sometimes. Step out of the box you are trapped in and try new things. Meet new people. Visit a new store. Try a new food. When you challenge yourself, when you stretch yourself—that is the way that you will grow, that you will stretch your brain and your mind! And when you grow, then you are asking your Warrior within to stand tall with you and stretch themself as well!

> **TO DO:**
> Write down 1 or 2 areas of your life you feel you have become stagnant in. What are some positive things you can do to challenge yourself in a safe way to wake yourself up?

Take care of your mind

Your mind is amazing. It has the ability to put you into a depressed state, but it also absolutely has the ability to bring you out and to have you feeling gloriously high, on top of the world, confident, strong, prosperous, and happy ... and to stay that way!

The mind is so powerful it can give us an amazing feeling of euphoria. But it can also create a fear so strong it can paralyze us from taking action. Fear is something that holds too many people back from really pursuing their dreams and living their life. The Samurai knew that fear on the battlefield could cost them their life, because it had the potential to either freeze them up, or affect their timing or skills. Obviously some degree of fear is a good thing. Be afraid of touching the stove if it is hot. But don't let it stop you from ever using the stove again. One of the things the Samurai worked on with their Zen master was to identify their fear, to get control of their fear, to master it. To use the power of their mind in a good way.

- Make sure you take care of your mind.
- Feed it properly, fill it with positive things that will help it grow.
- Challenge it.

- Stretch it.
- Never stop learning.
- Show appreciation for all that you do have; do not fill it with despair about what you do not.
- Do not allow worry or fear to permeate your mind.

As a Warrior chief once told me, there is no use in worrying, because by the time whatever you are worrying about comes ... the thing that you are worrying about will most likely already have been resolved. When I spend time in the acupuncture clinic, I find that this is the number one thing people complain of ... that they spend too much time worrying, spend too much time in a state of anxiety.

One of the lessons a Zen master tries to teach his student is to calm his mind, not to over-think, not to over-worry. When a Samurai Warrior speaks with their Zen master, the Zen master never answers a question in pure black or white, never states the obvious. He challenges the student to think, and to come up with his own answers to some degree. Are you challenging yourself?

The Zen master tells his student to continually work on himself. There is no set time to sit and meditate to the exclusion of everything else—he needs to continually stay in tune with himself and his thinking.

Your mind is your most powerful tool. Your mind can hold your Warrior down, or your mind can help your Warrior awaken to fulfill his glorious future. Be very careful of what you allow into your mind ... be aware of what you are thinking about and what you are focusing on. Nurture your mind, let it grow, and experience the amazing difference as you bloom with positivity and with confidence and you create the life for yourself that you want to live. It is within your control.

Remember, the Warrior inside you is waiting for **you** to come and fully awaken it and strengthen it. *You can do this!*

CHAPTER 4: Fueling Your Warrior Within

"The first wealth is health" - **Ralph Waldo Emerson**
"Let food be thy medicine and medicine be thy food" - **Hippocrates**

To fuel your Warrior within, the first concept you need to understand is that your body is an incredible natural healing machine. It is remarkably complex, and there is really nothing like it in the world.

In this chapter, we'll look at:

- How food and drink affects our bodies.
- Food and drink that will bring you closer to awakening your Warrior within.
- Food and drink that will take you further away from awakening your Warrior within.
- Potential ways to decrease the amount of pills/medicine you may be taking if you are taking medicine.
- What are you fueling your body with?

The 2-billion-year-old car metaphor

In Ewan M. Cameron's *The Osteoporosis Revolution: A Radical Program For Curing Yourself Naturally*, he explains the human body using the metaphor of a 2-billion-year-old car.

"Imagine that you are driving a 2-billion-year-old car. An all-natural, all-organic, living, breathing car. For 2 billion years, this car has been using fuel such as water, seeds, nuts, grasses, herbs, roots, fruits, vegetables, cereals, and most of these were eaten raw (not processed until all their natural goodness is totally and utterly destroyed...). That's the fuel this vehicle is used to.

Then, suddenly, after two billion years, that car switches over — for the last 100 years — to a new, modern mixture of: sugar, sweets, biscuits, crisps, 'fruit juices', chocolate, ice cream, coffee, tea, Coca-Cola, fats & oils, cigarettes, alcohol, pharmaceutical drugs, mercury-laden vaccinations, brain-deadening fluoride water, chemicals, pesticides, and preservatives, Genetically Modified Organisms (GMO), hormone and antibiotic-laden meats and milk (with any remaining natural 'goodness' destroyed by heat, a.k.a. 'pasteurization'), refined carbohydrates with ZERO nutritional value (white rice, white flour, white sugar, pasta, bread...), etc.

What do you think would happen to this 'vehicle'? That's right — it would break down. So you bring it to the mechanic, right? Now, is it in the mechanic's interest to resolve the SOURCE of the problem (your choice of fuel)? Or does he give you the 'instant fix' you need to get the car going again for a little bit? After all, you are a busy person, you've got places to go, you're experiencing pain and you are 'immobilized'. You need this problem fixed as soon as possible. So that's what the mechanic offers you: a 'fix'. Better yet: an instant fix. The car gets going again... but it's not going to last.

Think about this carefully. What should you do? What is the intelligent thing to do? Keep taking the car to the mechanic, or clean the fuel tank and use a cleaner fuel?

For every health challenge out there, all you ever hear from the doctor (the 'mechanic') is: take this drug or that drug. Simply go to Dr. Feel Good and pop a pill to make yourself feel all better again. Sure… take drugs to make the symptom go away ... But what about the source of the problem?"

This really hits the nail on the head with what is going on in society, and why so many of our Warriors are beaten down and stay hidden deep within ourselves, leaving many people just a shell of who they actually could be! Simply put, amongst other things, we are eating crap, drinking crap, and being prescribed medicines for everything.

Somehow we have gotten the concept of health backwards. Western medicine waits until we are sick and then gives us something to mask the symptoms, but very often does nothing to actually cure us or make us better. Wouldn't it make more sense to try to put all our efforts into *not* getting sick in the first place?

What are the obstacles to eating healthy?

One of the big problems with eating healthy over the past few years is that it has been challenging to find stores and restaurants that carry healthy options, and the cost of healthier food is often out of this world.

The *crazy* thing is that the healthier foods require less processing, but are often **more** expensive than processed and manipulated foods. How is it possible that plain old water could ever cost more than soda pop? Sure, soda pop has water in it, but also lots of other things such as sugar and chemicals ... and they all have to be processed.

Have you ever gone to a health food store and done some shopping? Depending on the store, it can be very expensive. But of late, things seem to be starting to change, and that is good news for all your Warriors. Good-quality food is starting to be made more available at more stores, and the prices seem to be coming down a bit. Besides, your health is worth the extra cost, and you could always cut back on another area of spending to afford healthy food, such as working or cycling to work once a week, which will save on petrol costs and improve your health and wellbeing.

How far has your food been shipped before it hits your table?

One of the challenges to healthy eating is how far is takes for your food to get to you. So much of our food is shipped in from very distant locations. Sometimes it is necessary, for example, maybe that food is not readily grown near your home, but in many cases, it's brought in from a far because supermarkets get a better deal on it. One of the problems with this is that with fruits and vegetables, once you harvest them, they start to lose their nutritional value. So if an apple is shipped from South America to Canada ... who knows how long ago it was actually picked?

The time and distance involved in the shipping lowers the nutritional value of the food, and it is hard to know what sorts of containers it might be stored in while shipping, many of which might house harmful toxins. Many of the foods have to be picked long before they are ripe, and so they are not allowed to grow naturally to their highest nutrition value. Plus many of the perishable foods have preservatives added to them, and sometimes there is no way of knowing what has been added.

So one of the things you can do is to avoid this is shop at local food stores when possible.

Stores that sell local products are often a bit more expensive because the stores are smaller, and they don't have the huge leverage and buying power that big chains have. But in those local stores, you can find local grown food and support local farmers. Try to go to the local farmers market to do your shopping and support them when you can, knowing that the food is that much more delicious.

In TCM, it is also strongly encouraged to eat foods that are locally grown. Your body is attuned to the earth in your area, and so food grown in soil closer to you will be more apt to have the nutrients that you particularly need to live in that area.

Eating out can be challenging

Options to eat healthily when you are out of the house are also sometimes difficult to find. In some countries, as you drive down a road to look at restaurants, you will see so many fast food places, burger joints, sub places, donut shops, and dessert places. And even the regular restaurants have menus filled with foods that are not very healthy (but taste good). Thankfully, healthier options are starting to appear on many restaurant menus. 15 years ago, if you went out to a restaurant looking for a vegetarian meal, the only thing you could eat was a salad and french fries! Whereas now there is a better variety to choose from, and things are improving.

On a personal note, I recently flew from England, and while waiting in Gatwick airport for a 10 hour+ layover, I wandered around deciding what to eat. I found a store that was a new idea to me, but that I loved. It was billed as a "health drug store". So it had all the regular drug store items, but at least a third of the store was filled with healthy foods, all prepared and ready to eat there or take on the plane with you. I was astounded! I got a great green drink there (with spinach, cucumber, apple, etc.) in it, a salad with falafel balls, a healthy snack bar ... and all for a price much lower than I would have suspected. I was in heaven! I took the salad with me on the plane, and it was such a nice treat over what the airplane food would normally be.

So there is hope! Things are changing! If you want to eat healthier when you are out and about, then tell the restaurants that you demand they offer more variety. If the demand is there, they will start to fill it.

Food is medicine

In TCM, the food itself that we ingest is the best medicine we can have! TCM is very preventative and all about balance. The food you eat can either set you and your systems off balance or it can restore you to balance. The concept of TCM is *perfect* for awakening your Warrior within! If you are interested in learning more about TCM and how food can affect your body, there is an excellent book by Paul Pitchford called *Healing with Whole Foods*.

There are some common questions on food we'll talk about now.

Should a Warrior eat organic food? Is it worth it?

It's funny, when you think about it, that this new, special phenomenon now called "organic food" used to just be called ... "food".

In general, our family tries to eat organic as often as possible. I am not a nutritionist, but to me it just makes sense to eat things that are as natural as possible and not have to worry about what each food item has been coated with to preserve it and make it as shiny-looking as possible.

Organic foods will often not look as good as non-organic foods. But does the fact that it looks perfect, with no blemishes and super shiny, outweigh the stuff they do to it? And if you do a **taste** comparison, organic foods taste much better.

What are GMO foods? Are they safe?

GMO stands for **Genetically Modified Organism**. Mmm, sounds delicious doesn't it? Let's take a naturally occurring food, something we have been eating for thousands of years, and fiddle with its actual genetics, and create a totally NEW food, something that is alien to our body. Nothing could go wrong with that ... could it?

GMO foods have created a real storm. Companies that produce them tell you of course they're safe! Yet how can they possibly know? They have been around for such a small length of time, can any study really show safety beyond a doubt?

Why did I become a vegetarian? Should you?

20 years ago, when I lost my health, when my body and immune system were broken down, when I was sick month after month after month, when I was physically and mentally exhausted, I decided to give up meat. This was a major turning point in my health, as my body seemed to digest things better, and overall I felt lighter and more energized.

According to the Mayo Clinic, three important potential benefits of eating no meat (or at least less meat) are:
- Reduced risk of diabetes
- Reduced risk of heart disease
- Reduced risk of cancer

If you are considering becoming a vegetarian, it is important that you do your research to ensure you are getting the proper nutrition that you need. Speak to your doctor or a certified nutritionist.

Some general tips on eating

These are things I have personally experimented with over the years that have really helped me.

1. **Fill at least half your plate with veggies** – Ok, so if you still love your meat, at least fill half your plate with vegetables. They can be cooked or raw. My favorite is lightly cooked so they are warm but still crispy (I put a touch of organic coconut oil in a pan and sear them very quickly). Different colored veggies can really light up your plate and your body will definitely thank you for them!

2. **Try organic food** – We just looked at the benefits of organic ... so if you can add some organic food into your diet, it can only help. My wife (who is not vegetarian) went through a period in life where she felt very "fuzzy" in her brain, unfocused, and found it hard to concentrate. She made a couple of tweaks to her diet, and one major change was to buy **only** organic chicken, and it was amazing to see how quickly her "fuzziness" disappeared! Be warned that for the most part, organic foods are more expensive than regular

foods. As always, we have choices to make. I suggest you at least give it a try and see whether you notice a difference in how you feel. If it turns out to be a major ingredient in improving your health, then it's worth a few extra bucks.

3. **Eat every three hours** – This was a principle I finally paid attention to when introduced by one of my mentors, Joel Bauer. Joel took himself from overweight and unhealthy to feeling very good, and this was one of the key concepts he learned to do. You will find that if you eat every 3 hours, you will always top up your hunger. The times that we really eat badly are when we are famished, and so we overeat everything before our stomach has a chance to tell us it is full. Try this schedule out and see how it feels to your body. Note: If you are someone with a fast metabolism or diabetes, you may need to alter this schedule. If you have any questions, it is always best to check with your doctor.

4. **Have food prepared and always handy** – This is *the* biggest tip to really keep eating nutritiously and avoid eating junk food. Always have good food with you in an easy-to-access format. Bring food and snacks with you to work, to events, on long drives, on hikes, wherever you go. Keep your food in re-sealable containers. Glass is good because it is very clean and does not leak toxins into your food as plastic potentially could. If you don't have good food with you and you get hungry, then that's when it is all too easy to eat a couple of donuts or other fast food. Preparation is critical. The night before is the best time to prep food (cut up veggies, cook sweet potatoes,

wash fruits, get almonds and berries, prepare veggie spaghetti, etc.).

5. **Drink more water** – Water helps your entire body; it helps your cells; it helps your body dispose of toxins. How much water should we drink? There really is no one answer. If you add even a couple of glasses (or bottles) of pure water to your diet each day, you will begin to feel a difference. Tweak it a little bit each week until your body tells you the perfect amount for you! If you sweat a lot, you will need to replenish more, so if you live in a warmer climate or you exercise, you may need to drink more than someone else. As well, if you are suffering from conditions where your body is losing a lot of liquid (such as vomiting or diarrhea), you may need to replenish it more frequently.

Is there such a thing as too much water? Yes. There is a condition called hyponatremia where if you drink too much water, your kidneys cannot properly deal with it. As a guideline, generally drink just enough water so that you do not feel thirsty. If you are concerned with your water intake, consult your doctor or a registered nutritionist.

6. **Drink less soda pop** – Ideally, you should just stop drinking soda pop entirely, but if you are someone who is somewhat addicted to it, it can be a battle to drop it entirely. The crazy thing is that even though you know how bad it is for you, you can still sometimes crave it.

Do you know how much sugar they put in a regular cola for example? One brand put in thirty-nine grams. That is the equivalent of approximately 9 1/2 cubes of sugar! Can you imagine pouring a drink out and then consciously adding 9 1/2 sugar cubes, one after another? Even with "diet" soda, many use the artificial sweeter aspartame, and there are numerous studies that suggest aspartame can have harmful effects on your body.

7. **Stop drinking cow's milk and try almond milk instead** – Many people are lactose intolerant, and may be suffering from side effects such as abdominal bloating, pain, diarrhea, gas, or nausea to name a few. In addition, cow's milk is mostly mass-produced, and the cows are often fed all kinds of antibiotics, and so you may be drinking those when you drink your milk.

   I had massive problems with sinus infections for years, and so in my early research, I discovered that some studies suggest cow's milk might be aggravating it. There's not a huge amount of evidence to support it at the moment, but I decided to try it regardless. Since I have stopped, my body in general functions better.

   Almond milk is a viable healthy substitute for cow's milk. It is low in fat, but high in energy, proteins, lipids, and fiber. It contains some good vitamins and minerals as well.

8. **Try juicing** – Juicing is a great way to add the benefits of fruits and vegetables into your diet quickly and easily. It can also help your body detoxify. The documentary "Fat, Sick and Nearly Dead", shows how Australian entrepreneur Joe Cross was able to reset his body, get himself off his prescription meds, and lose a lot of weight, by adding juicing into his life. Of course, just like anything, moderation is important, so include it

as part of your balanced diet, and consult your doctor or nutritionist if you have any questions or concerns

There are many different types of juicers and many different prices. You can do some research and see which one fits your budget. One word of caution, however. There are "juicers" and then there are "mixers". Juicers do exactly what they sound like: they extract the juices from whatever you put in, so it is a liquid like apple juice.

Mixers, on the other hand, produce something that is heavier, like a smoothie. The most popular brand I have heard of is Vitamix, and many owners of Vitamix swear by it. I found the "mixer" to be too heavy, it was more like a meal, so that is why we got a juicer. And we are very happy with our decision.

Some handy tips on *how* to eat

- **Sit down to eat.** Remember the concept of fight or flight vs. rest and digest. It you are running around while you eat, your body had its energy diverted from your digestive system, and so you lose out on nutrition. So sit and relax while you eat!
- **Chew food well.** This allows your stomach to be able to digest it better, and therefore get more nutrients out of it.
- **Pay attention to eating.** Turn off the television, get away from the work desk so you can be mindful, and have gratitude for what you eat.
- **Do not skip meals.** Skipping meals plays havoc on your body, and can lead to sudden desires for sweets and binge eating.

- **Moderation is key.** Don't allow yourself to get too hungry or too full.

The top 12 superfoods that can heal your entire body

Ewan M. Cameron's top 12 superfood choices are aloe vera, wheatgrass, sprouts, turmeric, nettles, Limu juice, Maca, goji berries, hemp, chlorella, garlic, and coconut. Personally, I also add ginger, quinoa, almonds, blueberries, organic coconut oil, and kale into our top rotation of foods as well. They have some great health benefits, so try some of these, little by little, and see which ones you prefer. Then add them to your diet!

Some other great food choices

There are some other food/food ideas I have found that you may love and that have great benefits.

Vega - Vega is a meal replacement/protein drink that I use, developed by a vegan triathlete named Brandon Brazier. It has 20 grams of protein per serving, and you just add to water, so it is low in calories, and it tastes good (I like French Vanilla the best). But most importantly, it contains a lot of essential things I would never get in my diet otherwise. While I have no scientific proof of this, I credit Vega with helping me win back and solidify my immune system and ability to fight off colds when all around me are sick (whereas before, I would get sick if someone with a cold even talked to me over the telephone!).

Almond butter - This is a great substitute for the commercial peanut butters. Our whole family loves it. A very uniquely delicious combo to try is raw celery sticks with almond butter (in the groove). It may sound "different", but you may really fall for it!

Squirrelly bread (by Silver Hills Bakery) - This is a bread (found in the frozen section) that is non-GMO, and made from organic whole sprouted wheat. One of my favorite sandwiches I read about in Brandon Brazier's Cookbook is Squirrelly Bread bagels, with tons of sprouts and avocados.

Kombucha - I use this as a replacement for pop, in particular for the fizziness of pop. It is a fermented tea drink filled with vitamins, enzymes, and probiotics, and can have positive effects such as helping with digestion, boosting energy, strengthening the immune system, and more.

Green tea - Many people say that green tea is much healthier for us, has antioxidant properties, and some even claim it can help with weight loss.

Coconut water - This is another great pop substitute. I love the taste and find it very thirst quenching. It is packed with antioxidants, amino acids, enzymes, B-complex vitamins, vitamin C, and minerals such as iron, calcium, potassium, magnesium, manganese, and zinc.

Organic coconut oil - We use this for cooking all the time because it has some great health benefits and gives food an excellent, unique taste. If I am stir-frying my veggies, I put a touch of coconut oil in the pan and very quickly cook them, so they stay nice and crunchy!

Herbamare Original (by A. Vogel) - We use this as a seasoning for almost everything, soups, dishes, salads, etc. It is a sea salt containing herbs, vegetables, and spices. We never use regular salt anymore as Herbamare is better for you and tastier!

Quinoa - We use quinoa (pronounced KEEN-wa) as a rice substitute, as it is a very nutritious and a good source of vitamins, fiber, and protein. It goes very well with almost everything. We put it in soups, we use it with stir-fries, and it is also good cold with veggie salads.

Hemp hearts - I use this to sprinkle on salad, put some on my oatmeal, and put in smoothies. Hemp hearts are a complete protein and contain the essential fatty acids omega 6 and omega 3.

Organic oatmeal - If you want something hot and filling for breakfast, I have found organic oatmeal to really hit the spot. It is a great substitute for a traditional sugar-filled processed cereal. I add almond milk and a touch of organic maple syrup. You can also cook a combination of quinoa and oats; it's really delicious.

PUR sugar-free gum - This is a gum without aspartame or GMOs. I first saw it on a program called the *Dragon's Den* (the equivalent of *Shark Tank* in the USA). It has a good flavor, lasts a long time, and is a healthier alternative than chewing gum.

> Think about what you are fueling your body with. *Could you be doing better?* The answer is probably "absolutely yes".

So for most of us, we want to ensure we start feeding our bodies with healthier, more energizing foods. But you need to be careful not to get overwhelmed in thinking that you need to do too much at once. Remember, it doesn't have to be an all-or-nothing thing.

Just start in a simple fashion by making a list of things you want to change or experiment with, and then choose one or two things to try. But, try those things as soon as possible, today, or tomorrow at the latest. A simple thing to try if you are a coffee drinker is to switch one cup of coffee for something healthier such as a cup of green tea.

Ensure that you do not allow yourself to get paralyzed into non-action when looking at your list!

> **TO DO:**
> Once you have your list, then circle one thing, no matter how small it is, and do that thing, make that one change **right now**. Do not read another word. Put the book down immediately and do that one thing, right now! Change your life! You deserve to feel fully alive again!

CHAPTER 5: Moving and Rejuvenating Your Warrior Within

Movement is critical to ensure our bodies stay balanced and healthy. Your body also needs proper time to rejuvenate and recover from the movement. These are two areas we tend to ignore. If you are feeling down, de-energized, or depressed, then odds are that you are **not** doing this sufficiently. To awaken your Warrior within, it's vital that you add this into your daily schedule.

In this chapter, we'll look at:
- Why you need to rejuvenate your body.
- The negative effects of not sleeping enough.
- Some tips to help you improve your sleep.
- Some ways to get moving.

Why you **need** to rejuvenate

Throughout your day, whether you are driving your car, at work, studying, playing with your kids, doing yard work, thinking, or worrying, you are burning up energy. Your body and mind are hard at work. Just like any machine, your body needs some down time to recuperate and recharge its batteries. Eating a proper diet helps and thinking good thoughts helps, but you also need to give your body time to totally relax and rejuvenate.

When people practice Qigong or Reiki, or when they meditate, they are putting their body and mind into a state of rejuvenation. That is why they feel so energized, for example, after a Reiki session. It puts their body into such a deep and complete state of relaxation. Often, my clients just fall asleep right there on the table and wake up feeling so relaxed and energized!

It's important to give our bodies time to rejuvenate. When we go on vacation and sit on a tropical beach listening to the sound of the waves rolling in, we let go of all our worries and stresses—it's very rejuvenating. Being in nature, feeling the energy of the trees, connects with our bodies at the deepest level, and so it rejuvenates our bodies as well.

But the key rejuvenator—the key down-time tool that we have is a simple thing: **a deep, uninterrupted sleep**. Unfortunately, millions of people suffer from the inability to get a good night's sleep and therefore don't give their body the time it needs to rev up its engines. It is estimated that roughly 60 **million** people in the USA *alone* suffer from inadequate sleep. 60 million!

Negative effects of not enough sleep

If you don't get enough sleep, you wake up the next day feeling the worse for wear. It affects all areas of your life: work, relationships, family, decision-making processes, moods, mental health, and physical health. Many people suffer from insomnia, which means they just don't get enough sleep, and they suffer because of it. This needs to be fixed!

Fatigue makes cowards of us all

One of the major negative results of not getting enough sleep is that it wears down your **courage**. When you are tired, tasks that normally might seem fine now seem overwhelming. You might choose to put off certain tasks because it just seems too much, and tell yourself will do it "tomorrow". The problem is that if you are suffering from any type of insomnia that lasts more than one night, then tomorrow doesn't come. Things just build up, and that introduces stress into your life

Never make big decisions when you are tired

Because your whole mental and physical state suffers when you are tired, and because everything seems worse when you are tired, a good rule of thumb is to never make big decisions when you are tired, especially at night. You might take the easy way out or be filled with too much anxiety; regardless, when you are tired, you often view the outcome of your options as negative. And it is no way to start out making a decision if your mind is already seeing failure. You should always try to wait until the next day, until you have some positive mojo flowing.

If you don't get proper sleep in the short term, then you may:
- Keep hitting the snooze button in the morning.

- Be crabby at work and snap at people.
- Not pay enough attention to detail.
- Not be able to think as clearly as normal.
- Make bad decisions based on raw emotion rather than fact.
- Not be able to do things with your kids that you want to do.
- Not have the energy to really be with your spouse.
- Get lazy and messy around the house.
- Fail to prepare things the night before and so rush around in a panic in the morning.
- Swerve dangerously when driving, placing not only yours but other lives in danger.
- Take shortcuts in tasks, and not doing things thoroughly.

Tools and tips to help you sleep

Black out curtains - These are very thick, dark curtains, which essentially block all light from coming in. They can make an instant impact for you.

A fan for background noise (white noise) - For me personally, this is my number one sleep aide. I usually always have a fan on in the background when I am trying to sleep. If I stay over at hotels, I try to always bring a small fan with me in case they do not have one, or worse, if they have a unit that switches on and off all night.

White noise machines - You can download apps on your phone, buy CDs, or find videos on YouTube that just play a never-ending "static" sound. If you have never tried one, when you first listen to it, you will actually notice the noise, but after a few minutes, you will likely forget it is there. If you have to listen to a machine, listen to it via speakers because wearing headphones is often uncomfortable.

Ear plugs - These can be very effective in blocking out noises that might disturb your sleep.

Don't drink just before bed - If you fill up your bladder with beverages, you will more often than not get awakened by your own body telling you it is time to tinkle. If you find this troubles you, then try to not drink two hours before you go to bed.

Essential oils - These can be used for all sorts of reasons, including helping you relax and get better sleep. Some common ones that can help with relaxation and sleep are chamomile, lavender, valerian, and orange. Of course, as with everything, you should check with your practitioner to ensure these would be good for you and that you don't have any allergies to them.

Don't eat too much or too little - If you eat too much, then your stomach will be uncomfortable. If you eat too little, then your stomach may keep you awake telling you it's hungry.

Don't eat or drink things that stimulate you - Coffee, caffeinated tea, chocolate, pop, candy, all of these things can contain caffeine or sugar, which can stimulate your body and keep you awake.

Don't watch things that stimulate you - If you watch something that gets your adrenalin flowing, you may become too revved up to sleep.

Don't have a TV in your bedroom - The bedroom should be for sleeping. Train your body that when you go into your bedroom, it is just to sleep.

Don't use your phone or electronics in bed - The light from our portable devices is very bright and is very stimulating.

Let your pet go pee! - If you have a dog or cat that sleeps in your room, ensure you always let them out to go to do their business just before you go to sleep so they don't tap you or bark/meow at you in the middle of the night.

Exercise *yes*, but watch when you do it - Exercise can be critical to helping you sleep properly. However, you may want to experiment with *when* you exercise. Some people say that exercising close to when they go to bed is good because it gets everything out of their system and helps them sleep. Others find that if they exercise too close to the time they go to bed, when they get into bed their body is still pumped up and they just roll around restlessly.

Do something "mindless" before bed to de-stress - If you have had a stressful day, you will want to de-stress before you try to go to sleep. Some things that work for me are watching a mindless comedy show on TV or a game show, or doing a word-search puzzle (something that really doesn't require much mental power, as opposed to a crossword puzzle that makes you think), or ironing shirts. It will help you calm your mind. Reading fiction books can also be great, but don't read a book on business or something important because you don't want to stimulate your mind to start planning next year's goals.

Don't have important or emotional conversations just before bed - If there is something important to discuss (for example, about your future, or about your kids) try not to do it just before you turn out the lights. Instead, schedule a time earlier in the evening.

Get enough exposure to light during the day - Getting adequate light in the day is important because it provides a contrast to the night. Lack of light should be a clue to your body that it is time to go into rejuvenation state. So ensure you get enough light in the day for your body to notice when you turn the lights off at night. In addition, sunlight triggers the release of hormones in your brain. Exposure to sunlight is thought to increase your brain's release of a hormone called serotonin. This is associated with boosting mood and helping a person feel calm and focused. Then by contrast, at night, darker lighting triggers your brain to produce another hormone called melatonin. This hormone is responsible for helping you feel sleepy and go to sleep.

Melatonin - Melatonin is a natural hormone made by your body that is released when the sun goes down and darkness occurs. It plays a role in your natural sleep-wake cycle. Research suggests it can be helpful in treating things such as jet-lag or other sleep disorders that result from your natural biological clock (night and day pattern) being out of alignment. Some side effects of it may be daytime sleepiness, dizziness, or headaches. Check with your doctor to see whether this would be good for you.

A warm bath - Often, a nice, relaxing, warm bath will help your body relax and get ready for sleep. Try dimming the lights and using candles to create an even cozier atmosphere. You can also try adding a couple of drops of an essential oil like lavender into your bath, or using a nice smelling candle.

A back rub from a loved one - What could be nicer than a back rub from a loved one?

If you can't fall asleep, go to another room for a bit - If you get into bed ready to sleep, but you find yourself just rolling around, change it up. Go to another room for a bit, and think some positive thoughts.

Is your bed comfortable? - If your bed is too soft, or too hard, or if your pillow is uncomfortable, you may want to consider replacing it with something that is more comfortable.

Get evaluated at a sleep clinic - One of my friends went to a sleep clinic and found out he had sleep apnea, which meant he regularly stopped and started breathing throughout the night, which caused him to never feel refreshed after a night's sleep. He had to get a CPAP (mask with oxygen) and it really improved the quality of his sleep.

> Rate your sleep on a scale of 1 - 10, with 1 being "I have trouble sleeping every night" and 10 being "I always sleep deeply and soundly through the night". If you are not a perfect "10", then go through the list of sleep tips and see which one(s) you can try.
>
> **IMPORTANT:** only add one new thing at a time, so that you can accurately assess whether that new idea helps.

TCM says the critical time to sleep is 11 pm – 3 am

According to TCM, there is a specific time when you get the most rejuvenation out of sleep: between 11 pm and 3 am. Try your best to make sure you are asleep between 11 pm and 3 am, and see what a difference it makes in your life!

Food cravings and stimulants

When your body is tired, it starts looking for solutions to get energized. It will tell you to sleep to recover, but if you are at work and have a big presentation to make and you feel very tired, your mind starts working on you. That little voice in your head starts up, telling you that you need to wake up, by any means necessary. Often the solution it comes up with sugar or other stimulants.

Sugar causes high highs and big crashes

When you ingest a lot of processed white sugar, it quickly brings about a **high**, and you are energized and ready to go. However, what many people fail to realize is that the high will wear off in a few hours, and it will be followed by a **low** that will bring you even lower than how you felt before the high. So then because you feel yourself starting to come down from the sugar high, you pump in more sugar ... and then bingo you get high again ... only to be followed by a more treacherous low again! A sugar-filled diet can give you energy like that of a flare from a flare gun (bright but short), whereas a healthy diet is more like an eternal flame.

These highs and lows (which are caused by fighting between insulin and glucose levels in the blood) take a huge toll on your body. Your Warrior within functions best when your body is in balance. But as you can see, when you consume lots of processed white sugar in your diet, your Warrior is kept in a constant state of tug-o-war and it wears him down to the point that often he crashes. Then you need to do everything you can to bring him back to life. So be careful not to rely on sugar as an energizer ... it might end up having the opposite effect on you in the long run.

Other poor choice food stimulants

Caffeine is another natural stimulant and its stimulating effects can start as early as 15 minutes after consumption and last up to 6 hours. For many people, the choice of stimulants is coffee. Any time during the day when they start to feel a lull in their energy, they reach out for the coffee. It is huge at work; it has become huge at recreational events and even schools.

Caffeine can be found in many things, including chocolate, pop, coffee, and tea. Too much caffeine may have negative effects such as high blood pressure, insomnia, indigestion, incontinence, headaches, and even increased risk of heart attacks among young adults.

There are, of course, drugs that serve as stimulants, and some people choose to take these. They may feel great at first, but they too have highs and lows, and some of them are very severe. If you are looking to awaken your Warrior within, this is not the answer.

> Avoid the highs and lows of sugars and other stimulants.
> Balance in life is key.

Setting up your work day to rejuvenate yourself

There are some tips that can really help you be more efficient, more productive, and also still have energy left at the end of the day.

Do the most important task first

Brian Tracey's book *Eat That Frog* is about time management. He suggests prioritizing your tasks for the day, then picking the highest priority one and addressing that one immediately; get it out of the way early. We only have so much mental power during a day, and if you wait until the end of the day to take on a task that requires a lot of energy, you may find you are left with too little too late.

Strategically time-block your day for maximum rejuvenation

If you want to maximize your productivity, it is important that you plan your day strategically so that you can keep your energy up for the whole day. *The key is to make sure that you constantly refresh yourself.* A good strategy is to start your day with a 90 minute task, and work fully focused on that for the time period. Then—and this is the important thing—schedule a 30-minute **rejuvenation** time block. In this 30 minutes, you can do something that will re-energize you!

A very effective thing to do would be to do some kind of gentle exercise. You could go for a walk around the block, or do some Qigong exercises to get my energy moving. Listening to music is very invigorating, and so you can sometimes just close your eyes and listen to some great music. The key is that as soon as your rejuvenation period is done, you need to launch into your next 90 minute task, again with **full** focus.

> Make a list of the top 5 things you love to do that rejuvenate you, and make you feel alive. Now ask yourself... are you doing these things often enough? If not, then start planning ways that you can add them into your life. This is very important!
>
> Adding rejuvenation exercises into your life can make a huge difference in awakening your Warrior within!

Use time-blocking software

My good friend Matt Episcopo is a master speaker and helps give people the tools in life to get the "upper hand" so they can fully succeed in whatever they choose to do. He gave me some software called The Action Generator, which enables you to block off your time on the computer and tells you when it is time to move on to the next task or rejuvenation period. You can find out more about it on Matt's website: http://mattepiscopo.com/.

Eat for rejuvenation

What you eat while at work will greatly determine your energy level through the day.

- Ensure you eat breakfast so that you are not tempted to "snack" early in the morning.
- Bring you lunch with you as often as possible, including healthy snacks.
- Eat every 3 hours so that you never get very hungry. This point is really important, because if you allow yourself to get really hungry—that is when you will be the most tempted to fill your hunger with **junk food**.
- Do not allow yourself to get too hungry!
- Stay away from sweets such as donuts.
- Try to avoid heavy, fried foods at lunch.

- Try not to rely on coffee to keep your energy up.
- Really focus on bringing some foods that will rejuvenate you, that are light, packed with nutrients, and easy to digest.
- Veggies, fruits, nuts, and even a Vega shake are all examples of great snacks.

Moving your body

When things stop moving, stagnation occurs, disease occurs. Your body, soul, and spirit need to keep moving; your body needs to stretch, to exercise, to challenge itself and its muscles. Some people assume that when I say exercise or work out, it means they have to spend money and join a gym. Although a gym can be nice, by **no** means do you have to join a gym to get exercise.

When you move your body, it changes everything! It gets your Qi flowing, gets your blood flowing, kick-starts your mind, brings more optimism, more happiness. It is a powerful mood changer. Moving your body is an almost instant cure for anything! I know that when I am feeling down, that I need to get up and move, *especially* when I don't feel like it. If you are feeling down, if you don't feel like moving around—that is the **exact** moment you **have** to get up and move! Movement can literally transform your mood. And regular movement/exercise will make a huge noticeable difference in your life ... in every way.

Movement actually physically changes your body

You have probably experienced a **high** when you have exercised. This is not just something you have imagined; your body is actually making real chemical and physical changes! Your body releases natural mood boosters called endorphins, which can help you relax, feel good, improve your immunity, and reduce the perception of pain.

Exercise is that powerful! You can actually trigger your body to give you natural "feel goods", and you can do it whenever and wherever you want. You have complete control over this. You have this power!

Exercise is critical for strong bones

Something that not enough people realize is that your bones *need* forces put upon them to strengthen them. In other words, they need to be challenged or they will grow weak, and especially later in life may break easier. Even exercise such as walking, jogging, push ups, or lifting small weights can be very beneficial.

Exercises you don't need a gym membership for

Remember, exercise and working out doesn't have to mean you go to the free weights in the gym with the "big boys" and try to crank out such heavy weights that you get so sore you can't move the next day! It could be push ups against the wall, or squats.

One of the best exercises is something so basic and simple that most able-bodied people can do it. It is free. You can do it almost anywhere: in a park, in a mall in the winter, on a beach, in the city—it is good old **walking**. Walking is great because it is gentle on your joints.

Cycling is another exercise that is easier on your joints than running.

Rebounding is another exercise, and it has some amazing health benefits. Rebounding is when you jump up and down on a "miniature" trampoline. It is so small it can be done almost anywhere ... even in front of your television set.

Kettlebell – I was introduced to the kettlebell by one of my favorite push the envelope guys, Tim Ferris (author of The Four Hour Work Week). He did a little session on something called the kettlebell swing. It feels great, uses a number of different muscles, has some cardio involved in it, and will really give you a tight butt! You want to be careful that you do this exercise the correct way, so you should consult with a professional before you begin it.

Stair triceps raises – All you need is some stairs to do this exercise that will give your triceps a good workout. Stand backwards at the bottom of the stairs, and gently sit down on the third stair from the bottom. Then put your hands down on that stair, with your fingers pointing forwards, and push your body up off the step. Give it a try—it is a simple, cheap way to work on your triceps.

Swimming – Swimming is a great cardio workout, and it uses your muscles without putting a pounding wear and tear on your joints.

Find things to do on YouTube – There are some great exercise videos posted on YouTube. You can find things like: how to stretch properly, beginner's yoga ... and much more!

Start exercising: Are you exercising enough? Odds are you're not. It is time to plan how you will add some kind of body movement into each and every day. Remember it doesn't have to be hardcore all out exercise—it could be taking the stairs at work, walking around your block a few times a day... just make sure you keep your Qi and blood moving.

A very important concept here is to tailor the exercise so that it is something you can do. If your knees really hurt, don't do something like running that will put a pounding on your knees. If you feel you are really out of shape, then start with something nice and easy—don't push yourself so hard that you end up sore and not wanting to do it again. This should be **fun**! The key is to just do **something**, and do it every day!

CHAPTER 6: Energizing Your Warrior Within

"In every culture and in every medical tradition before ours, healing was accomplished by moving energy." – **Albert Szent-Gyorgyi, Biochemist and Nobel Prize Winner.**

So far, you have learned about the essential tools you need to awaken and keep your Warrior healthy and strong. In this chapter, you are going to learn the "secret weapon", which will really *supercharge* your Warrior! So I will share many tips I have learned and used over the years as I brought myself back to life. *Many people do not know of their existence*, but they are absolutely vital to feeling fully alive. Some you may have heard of, while some may be new to you. If they are new to you, you may find them "different" or a little challenging to believe in, but I fully believe in them as I have witnessed them and experienced them myself and shared them with others, who have also benefitted from them.

The tips in this chapter are actually very old, as ancient wisdom keepers and healers from several traditions had a keen understanding of energy and our energetic body. The healing traditions from China, India, Japan, and Tibet, as well as other countries all include the concept of energy, and how it travels through energy channels, or meridians.

In this chapter, we'll talk about:
- The concept of energy in our bodies and around us.
- Ways to improve our body's energy.

Energy in our bodies

Let's start by looking at the concept of "energy". Different cultures from all over the world have long believed there is an energy that flows through our bodies—that energizes our bodies. The concept is known by different names, and although they may differ slightly, there are many similarities. In China and TCM, it is known as *Qi* (pronounced *chi*). In Japan, it is *Ki*. In India, it is *Prana*. In western culture and in Reiki, it is known as *vital energy* or *universal energy*. In this chapter, I will refer to it as universal energy or Qi.

When I first lost my health and crashed to one of my lowest points in my life, I was not very open-minded about such a "crazy" thought as energy in my body. When my friend first brought up the idea of seeing her for an "energy" session, I honestly almost threw her flyer away, thinking of it as simply strange and a waste of my time. But because I was in such a bad way, physically, mentally, and spiritually, I decided to try **anything** as I felt I really had nothing to lose. In the first energy session I attended (Reiki), I actually *felt* energy moving up and down my body. It was not scary; it just felt cool, and it was very fascinating. After just that one experience, I was **hooked**! I was filled with a sense of wonder, a sense that there was more out there in the world than I was led to believe by western culture. And as I drove home, I felt calmer, things seemed clearer, the world just seemed to be moving at a slower speed, and I was more in control. It was strange, but it was relaxing; it was nice.

Have you had an experience of the energy flowing through your body yet? If not, are you open to it? I hope so, because it really does have the power to supercharge your life!

What is Qi or universal energy?

Qi is an energy that literally circulates throughout your body constantly through energy passageways called "meridians". In fact, your body is made of Qi. You are Qi. We are all born with a certain amount of Qi, called prenatal Qi. But we also gain new Qi from the food we eat, the water we drink, and the air we breathe. When our body is healthy, the Qi flows smoothly, like a beautiful untouched river, sparkling, light, and alive. People can sense your Qi; sense your energy.

However, illness or disease occurs when there is a break in the free flow of Qi. For example, if you are experiencing a lot of stress and it builds up, the stress can disrupt the flow of Qi. Picture that the once beautiful free-flowing river suddenly has a dam put in the middle and the water is stopped from moving. This lack of movement can create stagnation, and what was once pure, clean, flowing water, now becomes dark, muddy, smelly water. To get the river clean, sparkling, and light again, you need to remove the dam and allow the water to flow freely along its course. The same is true of our bodies, minds, spirits, and Qi. The health of your Warrior within, and therefore your health, is directly affected by the strength and balance of your Qi. But the great thing is that you have complete control over your Qi. Just as you can deplete your Qi and therefore cause illness, you can also strengthen and maintain your Qi at a higher level and increase your health.

> **How to sense (feel) your own energy (Qi/universal energy):** Place your left hand in front of you, palm up and fingers spread out wide. Now take your middle finger of your right hand and place it about 1/4 inch above your left palm. Slowly move your finger in a circle around your palm. Can you feel a sensation? It may feel like a gentle blowing on your palm; it may feel like a little static electricity on your palm, it may feel a little cool or a little warm. It may help you to better sense it if you close your eyes. Now slowly move your finger away a tiny bit and start to move it around again. Can you feel it from this distance?

Energy is all around us

You have most likely experienced the feeling of energy in your everyday life, but not been aware of it, or not known what it was. You can feel it in yourself. You can feel it in places you visit. You can feel it in other people.

Positive energy

Have you ever walked into a room and it instantly felt it was relaxing and warming? That it made you feel like just sitting down, putting your feet up, and just absorbing the atmosphere? If so, that's a room with some good positive energy in it.

Have you ever met someone for the first time and were just instantly drawn to them? Their back may even have been turned to you, and you couldn't even see their face, but still you sensed there was something about that person that you liked? That innately you feel they are a good person? That person most likely has some great positive energy around them.

> **Try to sense someone else's energy:** Stand about 6 feet away from a friend or loved one. Both of you need to put your hands out to your sides about chest height. Now, slowly move towards each other. Tell your partner the moment you can sense them, sense their energy. Often, it will feel it as if you are walking into a wall of energy, like a gentle electric field. What you are feeling here is the other person's aura. Some people's auras will extend quite a distance from their body. See how far away from the other person can you stand and still sense their energy field.

Energy from afar

Have you ever "felt" someone's eyes on your back? Have you ever felt someone staring at you from across the room while your back was turned? Ask yourself, how could you possible sense that? The answer is they are focusing their personal energy field on you, and your energy field is unconsciously picking it up.

Personal space

Have you had someone, even if you like them, come a little too close to you, and you back up or ask them to move back a bit, because it feels like they are intruding? Have you ever felt like you just needed some personal space? We all have energy, not only in our bodies, but around us as well; you can think of it like a force field. Many people call this energy field that extends around us an "aura". When I treat people in Reiki, I actually work much more in someone's aura than their physical body, that is, the energy field around them, with the knowledge that their aura will also connect with the Qi in their body. You can sense people's auras. If someone has a strong aura, those are the people you feel even from yards away.

> **Try to see your own aura:** Hold your hand, with fingers spread wide, away from your face at eye level, preferably against a dark or white wall. Now just stare at your hand, let your eyes relax. You may find that you start to see a whitish glow around the outline of your hand. This is your aura.

Negative energy

Have you ever walked into a room and the hair on the back of your neck just stood on end, and you felt cold or uneasy? That means there is some left-over negative or bad energy in that room. Let's say that you and your loved one are looking for a house to buy. You go into a house and as you walk into one room, you are immediately struck with an intensely bad feeling. It really gives you the creeps, and you feel like you just have to get out of there. After you have finished looking at the house (which was a nice-looking house in a nice area), you both immediately tell each other that you don't think it is the house for you. When you quickly share why you thought that, it turns out that you both got the bad feeling and left very quickly as well. You didn't know the other had gone into that room, but you both individually felt it very intensely.

Energy in nature

One of the most beautiful places to feel the power of positive energy is when you are in nature. Find a park or conservation area near to you and go for a long hike, or walk the dog, or go for a bike ride there. The energy in nature is very enlivening. There are many trees and flowers, and they all give off a nurturing, energizing, loving energy. This energy will fill you with peace, and because it relaxes your body at such a deep level, your body starts to rejuvenate and becomes energized.

Your Warrior needs you to connect to nature whenever possible. If there is a lake nearby, go and absorb the energy of the water and the wind. If you have a park near you, go and sit in the grass and breathe in the energy of mother earth. Even if the best you can do is a little front garden or even a single tree, go and enjoy it. In the cold of winter, one place you can go to for some summer weather is a green house. They often have all sorts of tropical plants, such as palm trees, that can give you the energy fix you need and make you feel great!

The energy is nature is real, it is powerful, and you need to let it be a part of your life. Just suspend your disbelief, let yourself go, and allow your Warrior within to absorb it and recharge.

How does it feel when your Qi is healthy and balanced?

When your Qi is sufficient and well-balanced, you know it ... you feel on top of the world. You feel energized and self-confident. You are healthy and able to fight off colds and the flu. You are able to make decisions and keep a quiet calmness around you even when all is chaos around you. You feel like a leader, like you are able to naturally take control of situations as you choose. You are comfortable in your **own** skin. You do not feel the need to be anyone else, and you do not feel the need to gain approval from others. You walk into a room, you have a presence about you, people naturally gravitate toward you ... including that potential person of your dreams! When your Qi is in balance, you feel good, and good things tend to happen.

When your Qi is low or unbalanced ... you also know it! You will feel unbalanced. You may feel tired, worn out, lethargic, apathetic. Your body will be out of whack; you will be more susceptible to falling ill; you may have a cold, the runs, stomach cramps, or acid reflux (heartburn). Your emotions could swing from depression to elation, and you could feel unstable.

What causes your Qi to stagnate, stop flowing, or deplete?

The lifestyle of "modern day" people is the number one cause of depleting your Qi. Too many people are always on the go, never stopping to take a deep breath, nor rejuvenate their bodies. They eat on the run. They are glued to cell phones and computers. Less time with their family, less time in nature.

Stress and stress-related illnesses are one of the biggest, if not the biggest causes of disease today. And stress is caused by so many things.

Food - Human beings used to eat food that was natural. Vegetables were grown locally. Today, we often ship our vegetables thousands of miles, with many of them losing a lot of their nutritional value by the time we get to them. They were organic, meaning pesticides were not poured all over them. Animals were also raised without drugs and slaughtered in the local area. There were not GMO seeds; there was not artificial, nutrient-robbed food. The food we eat nowadays is often empty of nutrition and loaded with "poisons". It is also loaded with bad fats, which clog up your arteries and body. Just like throwing trash into a water way will clog up the water, so will these things clog up your blood and your Qi.

Beverages – When one of the cheapest thing you can buy is pop (soft drinks), when they are often cheaper than water itself, you know something is wrong with the world. The overload of sugar and chemicals plays havoc with our bodies and our Qi.

Drugs - Prescription drugs are so frequently used for so many ailments ... and these trample down your Qi. It is amazing how many drugs are pushed out to people. Obviously, some prescription drugs are important; however it seems it has got to the point that for any little ailment we get, any condition, no matter how small, drugs are given. The pharmaceutical companies are **huge** players in this world. Their quest for profit drives the prescription and usage of these drugs. Some superbugs are now impervious to our antibiotics and so new ones must always be produced. Look at the list of side effects for many of the drugs you see advertised on TV. It is actually very frightening to see all the things that could go wrong with your body (some side effects include death!).

Pollution - Air pollution, water pollution, noise pollution—all these disrupt the flow of your Qi. All of these things clog up your energy channels disrupting the flow of Qi. Additionally, stress causes your body to tense up, and your blood vessels to constrict, which again slows down the flow of Qi.

Skin products - Many of the products people put on their skin and hair have ingredients that are not healthy for us, and they are often absorbed right into our bodies via the skin. The David Suzuki Foundation reported on a study that, "one in eight of the 82,000 ingredients used in personal care products are industrial chemicals, including carcinogens, pesticides, reproductive toxins, and hormone disruptors".

Cleaning products - Many cleaning products contain toxins and other things that are harmful to our health. Although you don't ingest these products, if you touch the cloth you use, it can be absorbed into your system through your skin. If you are using products with strong fumes, these are inhaled into your system, and can agitate or harm your lungs.

If you want to learn more about how the everyday products we use can have a detrimental effect on your health, you can read

Rick Smith and Bruce Lourie's eye opening books: "Slow Death By Rubber Duck: How the Toxic Chemistry of Everyday Life Affects Our Health" and "Toxin Toxout: Getting Harmful Chemicals Out of Our Bodies and Our World".

Lack of exercise - People used to have to walk to get places, chop fire wood to burn for heat, and tend to their crops. When you move your body, you get your blood and Qi flowing freely. Now people can sit in their house and with the click of a button have pretty much anything their heart desires delivered to their front door without having to get up off the couch. Kids used to play outside to keep themselves occupied; now they can live a very sedentary lifestyle playing video games and talking with friends on social media.

Too much stimulus - There is just too much information bombarding us, constantly attacking and stimulating our brains. People seldom give their brains a chance to just relax and recuperate. When the mind is always "on", it depletes our batteries; it depletes our Qi.

When my body broke down and gave up, although I did not know it at the time, I had *exhausted* my Qi to a very low level. It had become so unbalanced because I was stressed, working too much, eating crappy food, not exercising, not sleeping enough, not taking time to rejuvenate myself. So the years after, doing things like Reiki, switching to being a vegetarian, learning Tai Chi, getting acupuncture, and taking the time to rejuvenate—I was restocking my supply of Qi.

Building up and strengthening your Qi will be one of the main factors to awakening your Warrior within!

What increases, strengthens, and balances Qi?

The great news is that there are lots of things you can do to start increasing, building up, and balancing your Qi. You may find that you are quite depleted, much more than you realized. Regardless of how low or high your Qi is, you can absolutely change this and start the exciting and energetically vibrant climb to feeling fully alive—**super-charging** your Warrior within!!

Deep breathing - This is a simple thing you can do right now and begin to feel a difference almost instantly. Remember that all too often in life as you are rushing around, you end up taking very shallow breaths from your chest; they don't even serve to fully inflate your lungs. So stop for a second, place your hand over your belly, and really fill up your diaphragm with breath—make your hand move. By doing this, you will more fully oxygenate your blood, which gets both your blood and Qi moving.

Proper diet - A diet rich in healthy, nutritious food will help your Qi. Avoid foods that simply fill you up but have little value nutritiously. Avoid processed foods as they are often filled with bad fats and sugars, and are harder for the body to break down. As well, many of the nutrients have been processed right out of them.

Lower sugar consumption - Sugar is one of things that will keep our engines running faster and faster. It leads to high highs, and then an energy crash followed by low lows. If you need sugar, try to get it naturally through something like an apple rather than a chocolate bar.

Exercise - Exercising doesn't have to mean waking up at 5 am, doing a marathon, or lifting huge weights at the gym. Just move your body!

Meditation - Just the act of stilling your mind a bit, of trying to be present in the moment, will help a lot.

Qigong and Tai Chi - These arts for basic movement, breathing, and focus will get your Qi moving. There are many different types of each you can pursue; you can "taste" each one until you find one you really connect with. If you were to practice Qigong every day, it would have an instantaneous and power effect on you. (There is more on Qi Gong and Tai Chi later in this chapter).

Acupuncture - This is an especially powerful tool to help re-balance Qi in the body. Very thin needles (often you do not even feel them or know they are in) are inserted into specific areas of the body. TCM believes that there are meridians, or rivers of energy, that the Qi moves through your body in. If any of the meridians get clogged and the energy gets stuck, then the acupuncture needles can help direct the energy so that it can flow freely, and in the right direction again.

If you have never tried an acupuncture session before, then find someone who is properly certified and that you feel comfortable with. Give it a try—you may be pleasantly surprised. At first, I was a little anxious about the idea of the needles, but found I was worried for nothing. It played a major role in helping me get over years of sinus infections. Acupuncture also helped my daughter's sciatica feel better almost instantly ... it was startling to watch. It also regularly helps my wife *get rid of migraines drug free!* Can it work for you also? The only way you will know is if you give it a try when you are ready.

A breathing exercise to clear out negative energy and replace it with positive energy

This is a great breathing/energy exercise that I use *all* the time! (There are many more I can show you at upcoming bootcamps). You can use this when you are feeling low on energy, a little overwhelmed, or have a heaviness about you.

1. Sit down in a chair, with your back straight, and ensure your feet are touching the ground.
2. Place your hands on your thighs, palms down, fingers spread out comfortably, really trying to feel a connection with your legs.
3. Next start deep breathing. Remember, don't take thin breaths from your chest; instead take deep breaths from within your diaphragm.
4. You can practice a few breaths by placing your hand on your belly, and when you breathe in, your hand should rise with your belly.
5. When you are ready, take a deep breath in through your nose, then slowly release it out of your mouth until your belly feels empty of air. As you breathe out, envision yourself releasing a gray cloud out of your body. *That gray cloud is composed of anything negative, anything you don't want to keep inside you. It could be worry, stress, anxiety, jealousy, fear, financial woes, heart ache, fatigue, boredom, irritation ... anything that is holding you and your energy down right now.* Let it go. Let it out. You do not need it anymore. Notice that when you breathe out the grey cloud, it leaves a void inside of you.
6. Now take a nice deep breath in through your nose. Really make your diaphragm expand to take in all that new air! Picture this new air is a beautiful, relaxing, healing colour. You may love using the colour bright white, or a glowing golden light. As you breathe it in, picture it filling the void that you just created, it fills it up and then overflows into the rest of your body.
7. Each time you take a breath out, let go of any stress, any worry. As you breathe in, allow your body to fill up with a beautiful colour light. It is so peaceful, so relaxing, but also so energizing.

After a few breaths, you start to feel your body glow! You are not only filled with this light and positive energy, but you start to emit it. People around you can feel it, they sense your change. They may even be drawn to you because of it. They want to be near things that make them feel good.

You can use this exercise pretty much anytime, anywhere. You can use it at home, in the car, at work at your desk. When you go out in crowds, if you feel a little overwhelmed by all the scattered energy around you sometimes, you can simply go to the washroom, and do some breathing exercises just to re-center yourself. It works amazingly well. Another time you might find it very helpful is if you are in a stressful situation. For example, someone I knew had to deal with irate clients a lot, and so during his break he would re-focus himself, spew out all the negativity he had been inhaling, and recharge his batteries with positive energy so he could go out and continue to give amazing service.

Qi and martial arts

It is believed by many that Qi is a huge part of many of the martial arts, and that to be a true martial artist, one must work on and develop their Qi. Qi can help a martial artist deliver a strike with more power, and better absorb/deflect a blow. There are many legends concerning martial arts masters who are said to have had such control of their Qi that they could throw opponents across rooms merely by looking at them.

In the martial arts world, those that focus on the development and use of Qi are termed *internal martial arts*. In contrast, external martial arts focus on physical exercises, fighting methods, and the use of weapons. Many martial arts combine internal and external methods. A lot of the martial arts revolve around the concept of proper breathing techniques and how the breath applied at the correct time makes a huge difference in the success of an attack or defense ... and mastering breathing is a big part of cultivating your Qi.

My family and I took martial arts years ago, and we used many of the same concepts, such as exhaling while striking. The focus and calmness (which I now realise is consciously balancing my Qi) helped me in many other aspects of my life, particularly by keeping calm, confident, and focused, such as when serving a tennis ball and when writing exams.

Tai Chi – relaxation and a martial art

In Tai Chi, you learn a series of movements called forms. The fact is that many of these movements—although they look pretty and graceful—are actually martial arts moves! So you can learn to practice Tai Chi for relaxation or as a martial art. Most people practice it for the relaxation aspects. If you practice it as a martial art, you will automatically get the health aspects too. Many people find that Tai Chi, although it looks very slow and graceful, actually gives your body a thorough workout, and will bring some sweat beads to your brow. This is partially because you are using muscles you don't use often, but it is also because the movements of Tai Qi are designed to get your Qi flowing freely.

Qigong - the ultimate way to develop Qi?

Qigong is something that I have been studying and practicing over the last few years, and I have found it incredibly rewarding. Qi = energy (life force) and Gong = accomplishment, or skill that is cultivated through steady practice. When you combine the two, it can be translated as *"cultivating energy"*. This is such an amazing thing for a Warrior! Qigong is definitely something you should practice in your mission to fully awaken your Warrior within you.

Qigong combines physical postures, breathing techniques and focused intentions. The physical motions and the breathing techniques of Qigong help your body to heal itself. Overall, it really gets your blood and Qi moving, therefore keeping your body as healthy as possible. There are also special forms that are targeted to heal specific organs, such as your lungs, heart, or liver.

There are different styles of Qigong, which can be classified as medical, spiritual, or martial. They all involve breathing techniques, mental focus, and postures, but they focus on different results. Some practices aim at self-healing, by increasing Qi, then circulating it and using it to cleanse and heal the body. Other practices focus on emitting Qi to help heal others. Some of the Qigong exercises you will find are very peaceful and utilize very gentle movements. Some of them will involve more activity, and give you a good sweat. Tai Chi is actually a soft internal style of Qigong. Kung Fu is a more vigorous, external form of Qigong.

Some of the many benefits of Qigong are prevention of injury, speedier recovery from injury, building athletic and martial arts power, strengthening the organs and vascular functions, reducing stress, and balancing emotions. We always do some Qigong at events such as our boot camps.

I have studied with Qigong teachers in person (including Sat Hon who has written about how he healed himself of cancer), and learned some amazing things such as series of movements (like katas or forms in karate), healing sounds, self-healing movements, breathing patterns, and medical Qigong to help heal others.

"The body is a self-healing organism, so it's really about clearing things out of the way so the body can heal itself" **- Barbara Brennan, author of "Hands of Light"**

> **TO DO:**
> Practice makes perfect. The more that you get to know yourself and your body, by doing things such as mediation, Tai Chi, Qigong, and Reiki, the more you will develop your energetic senses.

Reiki and energy

I became a student of Reiki almost 20 years ago now. I am forever grateful to my Reiki Masters Helen, Peggy Margarite, and Barbara. They filled me with a love and wonder of Reiki and its energy, so much so that I became a Reiki Master myself and have taught students to develop a love and wonder of the Reiki energy themselves for many years.

One of the things Reiki does is help relax the body at the deepest level. When your body is in a stressed state, it does not allow the body to recover and rejuvenate itself, which is critical in fighting off disease. A Reiki session is so helpful for people because it places their body and mind in a state where they can fully relax and allows their body to work on fixing what needs to be fixed.

My clients have told me that upon completion of their Reiki session they have felt:
- Relaxed
- Focused
- In control
- Confident
- Optimistic
- On top of the world
- Happier
- More patient
- Like things slow down and they see things more clearly
- Energized

- Ready to go

In Reiki, I always thought of "energy" as "Universal Energy" or "God's Energy". Regardless of what it was called, for me, Reiki helped save my life. No lie. No exaggeration. Reiki was the thing that helped me awaken the Warrior within me; it was the first thing that even hinted to me that he might be there buried deep under my illness, stress, depression, and sorrow. Reiki allowed me to discover that my body was composed of Qi. When I lay down on that table and Peggy placed her hands over me and began moving the energy inside of me, my life changed for the good, forever.

One of the most powerful experiences I have had with Reiki occurred when it was first discovered that I had developed an irregular heart beat (atrial fibrillation). They decided the best course of action would be to use a method called electrical cardioversion. This is a procedure in which an electric current is used to reset the heart's rhythm back to its regular pattern. The night before I was supposed to have my procedure, I visited my Reiki master for a session. During the session, I felt "something" happen around my heart area, like my chest clicked and then felt a little lighter. I had a strong belief that something good happened. At my hospital appointment the next day, they found that my heart had "magically" gone back into regular rhythm and they didn't need to do the procedure.

Chakras

Another concept in Reiki is something called chakras, which are swirling mini cyclones of energy. There are seven main chakras in your body, and when those get clogged (when Qi gets stuck), then that is when illness can set into your body. When people work with an energy healer, one of the main things they get done is to make sure that the chakras are spinning freely and the energy is able to fully move in and out and around your body.

When I feel the energy strongly, I know that something is out of whack, and the energy, or Qi, needs to be balanced, and so I set my intentions to balance my client's energy. Sometimes clients will feel heat, or cold; they may see colours; they may have images in their head. Many times, people fall asleep on the table, even snoring, and the beautiful flow of Qi allows their body to get some much needed relaxation and rest so that it can start to rejuvenate.

If you want to try a Reiki session for yourself, I suggest you look up to see any Reiki masters in your area, and then see whether you feel comfortable around them. If you live near me and want to try a Reiki session, please feel free to contact me.

Here is the Reiki Creed, developed by Dr. Mikao Usui, which fits right into a Warrior's life:

1. Just for today, do not anger.
2. Just for today, do not worry.
3. Earn your living honestly.
4. Honour your parents, teachers, and elders.
5. Show gratitude to every living thing.

You can see that this has some similarities to the Samurai's Bushido code.

Reiki has been a huge part of my life. It is beautiful. Anyone with caring intentions can learn it and work with the Reiki energy. I have seen and been a part of some truly amazing and inspiring things during Reiki sessions. Try it for yourself.

Science and energy

As Qi energy cannot be seen (while, for example, blood can be seen and physically studied), western science has been very hesitant to acknowledge the possibility it really exists. Increasingly of late, there is research being done it. One example is a study published in the *Journal of Acupuncture and Meridian Studies* titled "The Primo Vascular System as a New Anatomical System". The study suggests that the primo-vascular system is in fact the physical component of the Acupuncture Meridian System. In other words, they feel they have found the physical channels through which the Qi flows!

Nikola Tesla, a very famous inventor, engineer, and futurist stated that "The day science begins to study non-physical phenomena; it will make more progress in one decade than in all the previous centuries of its existence". It is exciting to think how the world will change for the better when the concept of energy is finally accepted on a more general level in the Western world.

Fill your body with good energy!

Just like you want to fill your body with good food and fill your mind with good thoughts, you want to fill your being with beautiful, healing energy. You are so fortunate that there is unlimited energy all around you that is available for your own personal usage. Just reach out and grab it. Slow down and breathe! Go spend some time in nature. Eat good quality nurturing food. Drink water to cleanse your body. Think good thoughts. Exercise; keep your Qi flowing. If you have never tried something like Tai Chi or Qigong for relaxation and energy building, try it! If you have never tried a Reiki session, try it!

Don't let the fear of the unknown stop you. Just because something is "different" does not mean it is bad. To not only fully awaken your Warrior within, but to *supercharge* it, dare to explore and try some new things! This is your life, your energy. Fill yourself to the brim with positively, supercharged energy, and enjoy it

CHAPTER 7: The Awakened Warrior and Beyond!

In this chapter, we will:
- Review the steps you must take to awaken your Warrior
- Design your ideal future
- Discover how to earn more money or attract your perfect partner
- Enable you to see yourself as the Warrior
- Look at thoughts to guide you in your new life
- Issue the *21-Day Awaken the Warrior Within Challenge*

There is a lot more inside of you than you realize. You are more powerful than you know. No matter how low you are feeling, how lost you are feeling, you can bring yourself back to life so that you feel fully alive.

When you awaken your Warrior within, it feels like you are putting your armor back on, like you are so powerful—riding your horse at top speed into battle, with the wind blowing through your hair.

Taking stock of where we are

We have talked about some powerful things you can do to awaken the Warrior within you:
- ✓ The way of the Warrior, and examined the Samurai Warriors and their code.
    - o Stand out and lead a lifestyle you are proud of
- ✓ Awaken your Warrior within SPIRITUALLY
    - o Identify your passion and purpose, and ensure these are woven tightly into the everyday aspects of your life!
- ✓ Awaken your Warrior within MENTALLY AND EMOTIONALLY
    - o Be aware of what you are thinking about; make sure you are focusing on what you want, not what you don't want. Instantly transform your state when you are feeling down. Laugh, be grateful, overcome fear, be present—live in the here and the now.
- ✓ Awaken your Warrior within NUTRITIONALLY
    - o Ensure what you are putting into your body is energizing and healing your body. Is what you are eating and drinking bringing you closer to your goal, or pushing you further away?
- ✓ Awaken your Warrior within by MOVING AND REJUVENATING
    - o Move your body daily, because when movement stops, stagnation and disease occur. Make sure you spend enough quality time rejuvenating and recharging your body. Balance is the key to life.
- ✓ Awaken your Warrior within ENERGETICALLY

o Qi flows through us and around us and connects us with every living thing. Keep your energy fresh and vibrant so that it is at the highest level possible. Get to know your energy, experience it, play with it; people will be attracted to your positive and uplifting energy!

> What things have impacted you the most so far?
> What changes have you already made?
> How good have those changes made you feel?

I have shared with you everything I have learned. You have all the tools you need to awaken the Warrior within you.

Make the decision

Now it is time to simply do it. Now you must make the decision to go for it. You must eliminate all other options in your mind. It is no longer a thought that "it would be nice to do it"; it is now a MUST. You must do this! You can do this. Make it the only possible choice.

There is a great story I heard years ago about a general who sailed his troops across the water to fight the enemy on their home shore. The enemy were big, strong, and had the advantage of fighting on their home ground. As the general looked into the eyes of his warriors, he saw something he had never seen before ... he saw fear in their eyes. He knew that fear in battle would get them killed. Once his troops got off the ships and started up the hill towards their foe, they all glanced back at the harbour to see their ships ablaze, on fire. The general had set all the ships on fire so that his troops would have no escape route. He cut off all other options for them. It all of a sudden became fight and win—or perish.

With that clear decision now made, the Warriors straightened up their postures, the fear vanished from their eyes, and they went on to victory.

The Warrior within you is waiting for you to make that decision for it. Be the general and burn your Warrior's "ships." Let it know you are giving it no other option. *It is time to change your life, it is time to awaken!*

The steps to awaken your Warrior

1) Make a decision—decide that you want to make a change in your life!
2) Forgive yourself—the past is the past; it cannot be changed.
3) Clearly define what you WANT your future to be—remember, the future is unlimited; it is whatever you can envision!
4) Ensure you have positive self-talk; utilize the power of positive affirmations.
5) Be aware of what you think about—concentrate on what you want, not what you don't want—where focus goes, energy flows!
6) Eat to nourish your body.
7) Read and study to nourish your mind; keep growing, keep evolving.
8) Exercise to keep your body strong.
9) Rejuvenate your body, keep your Qi strong.
10) Clarify your passion and purpose in life.
11) Ensure you weave your passion into whatever you do in life—this is **critical**!
12) Have a mission—always have a target, something to shoot for, clear in your mind.

Your new future

Your future is wide open. Your future can be anything you want it to be.

How do you want it to look? Never forget that your thoughts create everything that you are, and everything that you will be. Be very selective in what you allow yourself to think about.

Remember *you need to think about what you want, not what you don't want.* When you think of your future, paint a picture as clear, crisp, and detailed as possible of exactly what you **do** want!
You can update and revise this exercise as often as you like. If you are inspired by something new that you want to in your life, then add it to your list. The whole key to this is to get your mind working, get it dreaming, get it calling out to and attracting the things you want to attract into your life!

> **What does your ideal day look like? Go into as much detail as you can!**
>
> - What time do you wake up at?
> - How do you feel?
> - What are you excited about?
> - Look out the window, what do you see?
> - Who is with you?
> - Do you have a hot or cold shower?
> - Are you listening to music?
> - What do you eat for breakfast?
> - Are you working that day?
> - Where do you work from? Home? The office? The beach?
> - What smells do you smell throughout the day?
> - What snacks do you eat? How do they make you feel?
> - How do you exercise?
> - Who do you meet up with during the day?
> - Who are you proud of?
> - What are you grateful for?
> - Are you driving a car? What kind?
> - What clothes are you wearing? (Or are you wearing clothes?)
> - Where do you live?
> - What does your house look like?
> - What is your favorite thing about the house?
> - Picture yourself smiling.
> - Hear yourself laughing with joy.
> - Do you eat dinner at home, at a restaurant, with friends?
> - How much money do you have in the bank?
> - What are your plans for the future?
> - What are you most excited about?
> - What time do you go to bed?
> - How well do you sleep?

There are two very common things that people consistently ask for in life: money and true love. As you are designing your new life right now, we'll ensure these two subjects are addressed here. You can get anything you want out of life, and one of these (or both) may be on *your* wish list. If so, then you can make it happen Warrior!

Earning more money

If you want to make more money, then the main thing you need to do to is to raise your belief of how much you feel you are worth! Our "self-imposed" limitations are often the main thing that holds us back from earning and achieving more. And why should you earn more money if you don't feel you are worth it? Sometimes, the limitations stopping us from earning more money are real challenges, like lack of skills or certifications. But whether it's a lack of skills, certifications, or positive beliefs, these are all things you can change to get the job you want and to earn more money.

What limiting beliefs or problems are holding you back?

So, the first thing you need to do is spend some time introspecting and identify what limiting beliefs or problems are holding you back. Some of these problems may be real, such as needing to add something to your resume. For example, if you feel the only thing holding you back from making more money in your financial advisor job is that you lack additional certifications such as Certified Financial Planner, then take a course and get your additional certification. Just do it. Or, if you want to move from an administration position to an outside sales rep job that requires more powerful speaking skills than you currently possess, take a course in public speaking and practice presenting. Find out what skills you need to enhance to get the job you want and then do it.

You may also harbour limitations that only exist in **your mind**. Maybe you believe "I don't deserve to make more money" or "It's only other people that make the big bucks, it could never be me." You may even have beliefs stuck in the back of your mind like: "There's no sense in trying because I'll just fail anyway" or "It's not my destiny to succeed." The *absolute* truth is that this *absolutely* false! You were put on this planet to succeed, to prosper, to contribute to the world. You need to mentally snap out of this poisonous thought process. You'll remember this from earlier in the book ... you need to change your thoughts and actions—change your life.

From now on, the moment you find a self-limiting thought enter your head, **stop it** in its tracks. Get up, start walking, recite some positive affirmations silently or out loud. When you sit back down, change your posture, sit up straight. Change your breathing patterns—no more shallow chest breathing, take some deep cleansing breaths from your abdomen. **Reset yourself!** This is a powerful tool you can use at any moment, anywhere, for the rest of your life!

Another surprisingly common mindset that can hold you back is the belief that money is bad. When I was younger, I knew some people who seemed wealthy to me, and they all had very poor relationships and scattered families. In the back of my mind, I thought "I don't want to be wealthy because I want to have a happy family life." It wasn't until I met some wealthy people who had caring, loving, and close families that I was able to move past this belief ... and then things "just opened up" financially for me. I realised that money is not good or bad—it is about what you do or do not do with it.

There are actually many happy and healthy wealthy people, but they often prefer to keep their lives private, and so we don't hear about them. Also, sensationalism sells, so the media tend to only report news if it is bad, because bad news unfortunately sells more than good news. An all too easy subset of wealthy people for the media to abuse are celebrities. You will normally only hear about celebrities if they are cheating on their partner, getting a divorce, or sadly commit suicide or overdose on drugs.

However, it's important to realise that it is not money that makes you happy or not. It is about whether you are internally balanced, and congruent— if what you do at work matches your inner values—and about the sort of self-talk that goes on in your head. Indeed, many unhappy wealthy celebrities just need to reconnect with their true inner self—they need to awaken the Warrior inside of *them*!

Money is never the key to being happy or unhappy, but there is absolutely every opportunity for you to be happy if you have money—it is up to you to make that decision to align your life with a mindset of abundant joyfulness. So don't ever allow yourself to use the fear of being unhappy to stop you from accomplishing the financial success that you and your loved ones deserve!

Is what you are doing connected to your passion and purpose?

If you are currently doing something that doesn't connect with who you are or what you believe in, or is something that you have no interest in it, then you will never be able to put all of your efforts, skills, and soul into it.

For example, if you take nutrition very seriously and only eat high-quality, natural food, but you are a sales rep for a snack food company that sells food you abhor ... can you see how your job doesn't connect to your passion and purpose? What you feel inside, how you act, and what you say have to be congruent. If you are saying something in order to sell your items, but you don't believe in what you are saying ... people will see it and feel it. Then there is no way that you can succeed to your fullest.

You have two choices here: 1) modify your existing job or 2) look for something different. If you work for a snack food company, is there a possibility that you could promote something like their bottled water line instead? Or perhaps they are introducing a new "oven baked organic beet chip" instead of regular deep fried potato chips ... could you help lead the expansion of that new line?

As a financial advisor, I shifted my business more from stock picking, which really didn't interest me much, to a heavier emphasis on financial planning and retirement planning for people, which really interested me. Can you find a way to shift the focus of your job to something you find more interesting?

How can you add more value?

Whether you are a teacher, a painter, a mechanic, a data entry person, or a brain surgeon, you can always add more value. Focus on what you can give ... not what you can get out of it. If you mix paint for people who have scratched their cars, how can you make it more of a positive experience for them, how can you **wow** them with your service? When you provide amazing value, word will get around. This could lead to a raise for you, or you could be invited to become a company trainer to train others in what you do so well. It could lead to double the tips. It could even lead to a job offer from the number one competitor who sees just how magnificent you are.

Start your own business on the side

Perhaps you have a nice stable job with a good pension that pays the bills, and although you don't *love* it, you don't want to give it up. If so, there are many other ways to monetize your passion ... by starting a part-time business that involves working with things that get your blood flowing! (Just make sure your company doesn't have a policy against doing this). As an example, information marketing on the internet is a potentially lucrative business that anyone could do from the comfort of their home part time.

You might be someone who has a crazy busy life, loves cooking, and has mastered making nutritious meals in a slow cooker, so you could create a training video that teaches busy people how they can simplify their eating habits and allow their meals to cook while they are sleeping. If you have **any** kind of specialized knowledge, there is a market for it ... someone somewhere who wants to know it. This is a huge area that could fill a whole other book in itself, and I will discuss this concept further in future writing, courses, and boot camps. For now, two great books to get your minds thinking are *The Four Hour Workweek* by Tim Ferris, and *The Laptop Millionaire* by Mark Anastasi—both of these books helped take my journey to another level, and they could help you do the same.

The core basis of making more money is a simple realization

This important realization is that there is an endless supply of money out there. During my Warrior's awakening, the biggest thing I came to realize about money is that there really is an endless supply of money out there, and there are so many ways to make money. It really blew my mind. Having this realization will change your life. We live in world of excess, not a world of scarcity.

You need to develop a mindset of **abundance**. The main thing that differentiates those that have an abundance vs. those who have a scarcity is the way they view the world. Millionaires view things differently from others. They ask different questions. They have different hobbies. They realize that money flows to the place of highest value. It is a natural law. Money goes to those who believe they are worth it. It flows to those that who put the thought out into the world that they are open to receiving it. Try this affirmation: "I attract money from all sources easily and abundantly" or "I make $20,000 a month" or "Money flows to me." Money is constantly in motion; it is never stagnant ... and it will always move from places of low value to places of high value—from people who believe they are not worthy of it to people who believe they are.

> **Earn what you are worth this year!**
>
> It is totally in your control how much you will earn in the next 12 months. Believe you are worth it, add the most value into the world, and love what you do!

Attracting your soul mate

Remember that the law of attraction states you will get back what you put out into the world. You get what you think about. *So the first thing you need to do is define who your perfect soul mate is. Not who they are not.*

> **Begin by writing out everything that you want in a soul mate:**
>
> Do they like to go for long walks?
> Do they like to read books by the fireplace?
> Are they athletic?
> Do they like to travel?
> Do they want kids?
> What do they like to do?
> How do you feel when you are with them?
> Do they make you feel happy?
> Do they make you laugh?
> Make you feel safe?
> Where do you live?
> What city?
> What country?
> Do you live in the country or in the city?
> Is there a certain body type you are attracted to? Or does that not matter?
> What do they like to do in their spare time?
> Is it important to you that they want to play golf in retirement?
>
>
>
> **Remember, focus on what you want.** And then look at this list every day, read it out loud, and let it permeate into you.
>
> Here's the cool thing ... the more you think about exactly what you do what, you send that energy out, and you attract a similar energy to you.

If you spend all your energy replaying failed relationships from the past, focusing on what went wrong, on what you didn't like about your ex, then that is the very energy you will be putting out into the world. And that is the very energy you will attract once again! That is why some people keep going from one doomed relationship to the next ... they keep projecting the same thing over and over and over.

Secondly, as you yourself transform yourself, your inner Warrior will shine brighter and brighter. You will shine with a different light. You will be authentic. You will be at peace with yourself and the world. You will know what you want. You will be more confident. You will carry yourself differently. And you will become a stronger and stronger magnet. That is why you need to really ensure that your mind is focusing on what you want to attract, not what you don't want to attract.

Your soul mate is out there. The thing is that you never know when you will meet them. It may come when you are least expecting it, and it may not be the person you thought it might be. But be ready. Believe in yourself. When you meet someone who you think could be that special person, allow yourself to act, to go and say hello. Reach out, make a connection. If it turns out they are not to "the one," then you are that much closer to discovering who it is.

I truly believe that you will know it when you meet your soul mate, that you will sense it deep within you. I speak from experience, because I met my soulmate at a time I did not expect it, and I felt like the most natural, calm, and beautiful connection. It felt right. And it turns out almost 30 years later that it was!

The awakened Warrior and beyond: thoughts to guide you in your new life

- ✓ Be an unstoppable force in life! Be a leader. By you awakening, you are helping the world to awaken, one Warrior at a time.

- ✓ Do something that challenges you, that forces you out of you little box, do something that scares you. Stretch yourself. You soul wants you to evolve! Your Warrior craves new knowledge and new experiences.

- ✓ Get to know yourself. Listen to yourself. Listen to your soul. Trust your intuition. You know much more than believe you do, you just need to learn to listen to yourself!

- What are your passions? What purpose did you uncover earlier in the book? What are you meant to do in this life? Are you doing it? If not, then make sure that your new future features you on fire with passion, it features you living completely in tune with your purpose. You are so connected to it, it resonates with every cell in your body. If you can't jump into it immediately, what steps can you start taking today to make put yourself into position?

- Remember the powerful quote we looked at earlier: "Doing something you hate is not a living; it is a dying". Life is too short not to be living! Make sure your new life is something that excites you!

- Ensure that you are coming from a place of love, rather than fear. Fear is cold; it constricts us; it stops us. Fear is very limiting. Love is warm, love is energizing, love is **unlimited**. In a world of fear, there is not enough, there is scarcity, things are fought over. In a world of love, there is more than enough to go around, there is ample, things are shared with a smile. Whatever future you plan for yourself, do it from a place of **love**.

- Work on your mindset with a purpose. A mindset does not happen by accident. Be disciplined in your efforts.

- Live your life by your Samurai Warrior code: do the right thing for the right reasons, calmly show courage and bravery in all instances of life, show kindness and compassion to every living thing, be polite to others as a result of truly caring for them, be honest not only with what you say but also how you act, be a man (or woman) of honour, have this as your reputation, and be loyal to yourself and to others.

> Anything is possible in your future. Remember this. Because starting this moment, you will be creating your future. This is no past. There are no limitations. Ask the universe for what you want, and then open yourself up to and allow yourself to believe that it is possible for you to get it.

You *are* the Warrior you have awakened!

Throughout the book, we have viewed the Warrior as something deep inside you that will give you power and strength and courage and confidence. But what you will discover, as your Warrior awakens, is that **you** are your Warrior. Your Warrior is you.

Always ensure you remember this: you are the Warrior!

Be the Warrior, live as the Warrior, be the shining light today, and you will draw people to you, people who want to be around you.

Like any Warrior hero on a journey, you are going to be presented with new things. You can choose to see them as obstacles; things that will hold you back. You can get angry or bitter about them; you can let them cause you to feel fear and to limit you. Or you can choose to see them as new possibilities, as things that will challenge you to become more, things you have the opportunity to rise above, and by doing so, you grow and evolve and become a better person and a stronger Warrior. You can view these things from a place of fear, or you can welcome them from a place of love. You have complete control over how you *choose* to perceive things.

Things will not always be perfect. But never forget to love yourself, and to forgive yourself. Set up your game up life with rules that give you a chance to win. You deserve it.

> I want *you* to start to call yourself a Warrior! Get a pen right now and write out your name on a piece of paper: "_____ Warrior _____". You might be John "Warrior" Smith or Sue "Warrior" Wembley. Breathe it in. Feel it. Be it.

I call myself Tony "Warrior" Wolfe. I do it because it makes *me* feel good. I do it for me, not for anyone else. When I see it, when I say it to myself, it empowers me. I am a Warrior! I am inviting powerful thoughts into my mind.

You are doing what 99% of the world is not

I am so proud of you Warrior! You are doing what 99% of the world is not. They are too afraid, or too tired, or just can't believe it is possible.

As stated at the beginning, this is a critical time in the world; we are at a turning point, and by you awakening your Warrior within, you have helped the world start to turn upwards again. You are amazing!

I very much want to hear from you. I want to hear of your challenges, and your victories! I can always be reached through my website, and look forward to connecting with you. As I learn new things, I will share them there, and I know in the stories you share you will teach me things I have not even contemplated yet. The world is so exciting. There is so much out there.

> **To do:** Continue your awakening Warrior, and then pay it forward. Help lead others to the light so that they too can finally awaken from their slumber.

21-Day Awaken the Warrior Within Challenge

To really maximize what you have learned, here is your challenge:

Every day for the next 21 days, apply something new from the principles you have learned here. When you do this challenge, I have no doubt in my mind that you will transform yourself! And as a gift, I have prepared a special free gift for you—just head over to my website under the "Book" section and register free for the "21-day Awaken the Warrior Within Challenge".

Warrior! It is time to put on your armour, get up on your horse, and ride! Your time has come!

Wake up and enjoy life again.

Life is too short not to enjoy it.

You deserve it!

To contact me, and for new updates visit me at: www.AwakenYourWarriorWithin.com

www.ingramcontent.com/pod-product-compliance
Lightning Source LLC
LaVergne TN
LVHW051835080426
835512LV00018B/2887